THE KINGFISHER
ATLAS OF
EXPLORATION
&EMPIRES

Simon Adams
Illustrated by Mark Bergin

KINGFISHER

BOSTON

KINGFISHER

a Houghton Mifflin Company imprint
222 Berkeley Street
Boston, Massachusetts 02116
www.houghtonmifflinbooks.com

Senior editor: Simon Holland
Coordinating editor: Caitlin Doyle
Designers: Heidi Appleton, Ray Bryant, Jack Clucas, Mike Davis
Cover designers: Jack Clucas, Malcolm Parchment
Consultant: Professor Jeremy Black, University of Exeter, U.K.
Picture research manager: Cee Weston-Baker
Senior production controller: Jessamy Oldfield
DTP coordinator: Catherine Hibbert
DTP operator: Claire Cessford
Indexer: Catherine Brereton

Cartography by: Colin and Ian McCarthy
                 Maidenhead Cartographic Services Limited
                 Maidenhead, Berkshire, U.K.

First published in 2007
10 9 8 7 6 5 4 3 2 1

1TR/0207/SHENS/SCHOY(SCHOY)/128MA/C

ISBN: 978-0-7534-6033-7

Copyright © Kingfisher Publications Plc 2007

LIBRARY OF CONGRESS CATALOGING-IN-PUBLICATION DATA
has been applied for.

Printed in Taiwan

CONTENTS

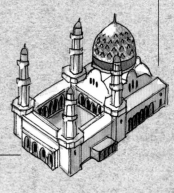

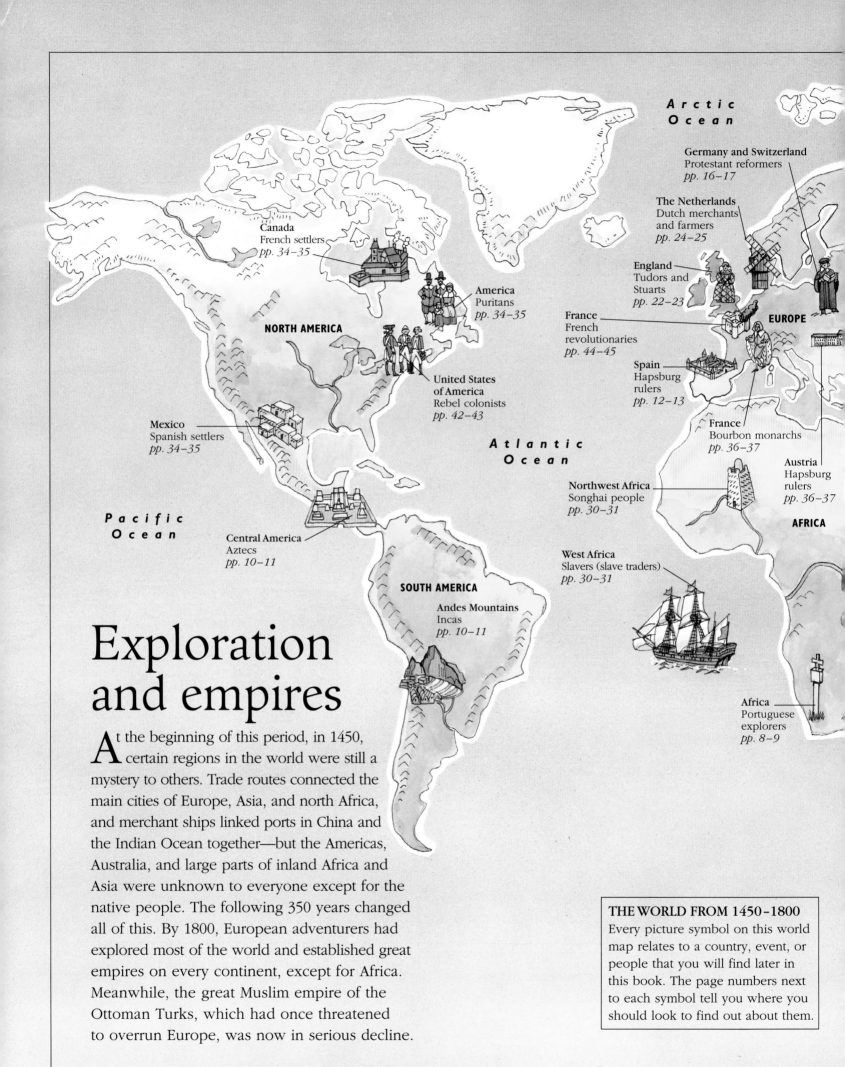

Arctic Ocean

Germany and Switzerland
Protestant reformers
pp. 16–17

The Netherlands
Dutch merchants
and farmers
pp. 24–25

England
Tudors and
Stuarts
pp. 22–23

EUROPE

France
French
revolutionaries
pp. 44–45

Spain
Hapsburg
rulers
pp. 12–13

France
Bourbon monarchs
pp. 36–37

Austria
Hapsburg
rulers
pp. 36–37

AFRICA

Canada
French settlers
pp. 34–35

America
Puritans
pp. 34–35

NORTH AMERICA

**United States
of America**
Rebel colonists
pp. 42–43

Mexico
Spanish settlers
pp. 34–35

**Atlantic
Ocean**

Northwest Africa
Songhai people
pp. 30–31

**Pacific
Ocean**

Central America
Aztecs
pp. 10–11

West Africa
Slavers (slave traders)
pp. 30–31

SOUTH AMERICA

Andes Mountains
Incas
pp. 10–11

Africa
Portuguese
explorers
pp. 8–9

Exploration
and empires

At the beginning of this period, in 1450,
certain regions in the world were still a
mystery to others. Trade routes connected the
main cities of Europe, Asia, and north Africa,
and merchant ships linked ports in China and
the Indian Ocean together—but the Americas,
Australia, and large parts of inland Africa and
Asia were unknown to everyone except for the
native people. The following 350 years changed
all of this. By 1800, European adventurers had
explored most of the world and established great
empires on every continent, except for Africa.
Meanwhile, the great Muslim empire of the
Ottoman Turks, which had once threatened
to overrun Europe, was now in serious decline.

THE WORLD FROM 1450–1800
Every picture symbol on this world
map relates to a country, event, or
people that you will find later in
this book. The page numbers next
to each symbol tell you where you
should look to find out about them.

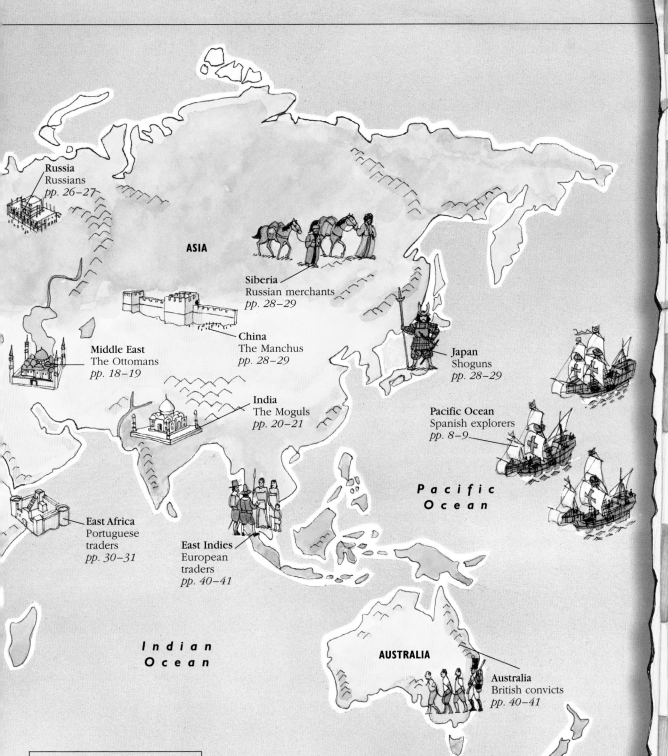

ASIA

Russia
Russians
pp. 26–27

Siberia
Russian merchants
pp. 28–29

China
The Manchus
pp. 28–29

Middle East
The Ottomans
pp. 18–19

India
The Moguls
pp. 20–21

Japan
Shoguns
pp. 28–29

Pacific Ocean
Spanish explorers
pp. 8–9

Pacific Ocean

East Africa
Portuguese
traders
pp. 30–31

East Indies
European
traders
pp. 40–41

*Indian
Ocean*

AUSTRALIA

Australia
British convicts
pp. 40–41

LOCATOR MAP

You will find a world map
like this with every map in
the book. This allows you
to see exactly which part
of the world the main map
is showing you.

KEY TO MAPS IN THIS BOOK

JAPAN	Main region or country
Deccan	Other region or province
■ PARIS	Capital city
● Yorktown	City, town, or village
Zambezi	River, lake, or island
Andes	Ocean, sea, desert, or mountain range
— · — · —	National boundary
– – – – –	Empire boundary

The world from 1450–1800:
What we know about the past

The world changed rapidly after 1450. Inventions that had been known to the Chinese for a long time, such as printing and gunpowder, transformed the world when Europeans discovered them for themselves and then exported them to other continents. New ship designs and navigational aids helped European adventurers explore and then conquer a lot of the globe. In some countries systems of government based on the rule of an emperor or king were gradually replaced with "democratic" rule by the people, although democracy of this type would not be widespread until the late 1800s. Not everyone was affected at the same time or at the same speed by these changes, but the world of 1800 was very different than the world of 1450.

Printing

In the German town of Mainz, in 1448, Johann Gutenberg developed a printing press that used movable type. This led to a revolution in learning, because more and more people were able to obtain and read printed books and pamphlets on a wide range of subjects. It also allowed new or revolutionary ideas to circulate freely as they never had before. Gutenberg's first printed book was the Bible (above).

Democracy

The intellectual revolution of the 1700s—known as the Enlightenment—led many people to question how they were governed and to seek to govern themselves through a democracy. By 1800, democratically elected parliaments ruled some western European nations, as well as the United States of America. The picture above shows the United States' Declaration of Independence, which was signed in 1776.

Powerful monarchs

After 1640, a series of powerful kings ruled in Europe. They were known as "absolute monarchs" because they believed that they held complete power and did not have to answer to anyone else on Earth. One of the most powerful of these kings was Frederick the Great of Prussia (ruled 1740–1786), who ordered the construction of the Neue Palais (below) in Potsdam, outside of Berlin, in Germany.

The Neue Palais was built from 1763–1769 to celebrate Prussia's successes in the Seven Years' War (1756–1763) against Austria, France, and Russia.

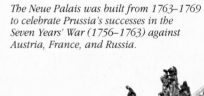

Palace contains more than 200 rooms, including four state reception rooms

New forms of warfare

Gunpowder was known to the Chinese and possibly to the Arabs by the 900s, but its use in Europe from the 1300s onward revolutionized warfare. European armies used gunpowder to fire lead bullets from rifles and muskets. Armed with these weapons, they easily overwhelmed their opponents, helping them conquer large parts of the globe by 1800.

Early 17th-century European wheel-lock pistol

Exploration

European navigators began to explore the rest of the world after 1450, discovering the American continents and a new sea route to Asia around the south of Africa. These voyages allowed Europeans to dominate world trade and set up colonies on every continent. In this picture Dutch merchants are trading with Native Americans in what is now New York City.

More than 400 sandstone statues, mass produced by a team of sculptors

Southern wing contains Frederick the Great's apartments and a small theater used for operas

Statues of the Three Graces (Beauty, Mirth, and Good Cheer) support the Prussian royal crown.

Voyages of discovery

In the mid-1400s European sailors explored the oceans in search of trade, wealth, and conquests. The Portuguese led the way, exploring the coast of Africa and discovering a sea route to India and Asia. The Spanish sponsored (financially supported) Christopher Columbus to find a western sea route to Asia. Instead, he found the Americas. The English and French then looked for a northwest route to Asia around the north of North America, while the Dutch looked for a northeast route around Siberia. By 1600, Europeans ruled the seas.

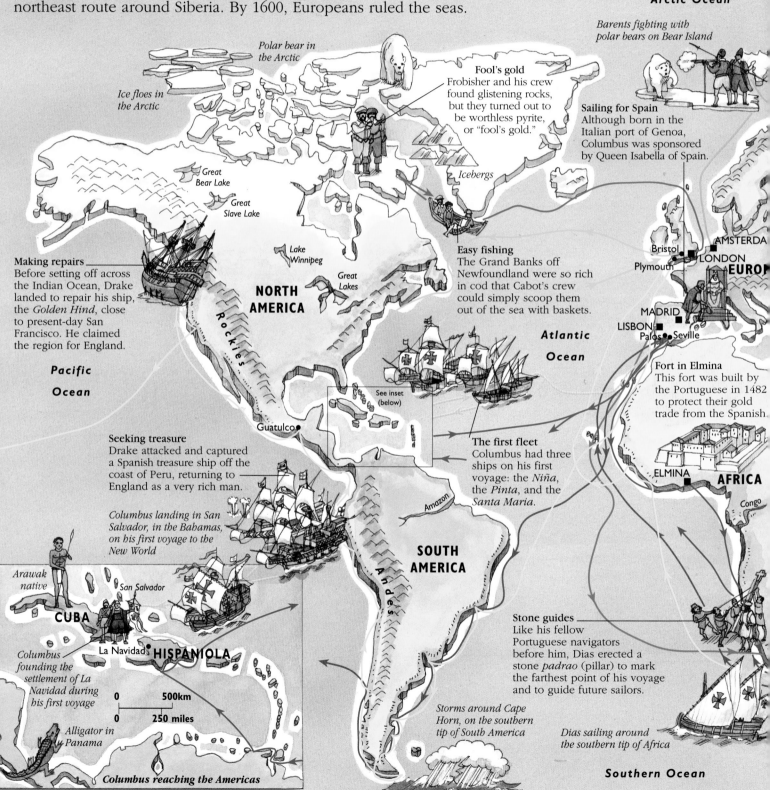

Arctic Ocean

Polar bear in the Arctic

Ice floes in the Arctic

Barents fighting with polar bears on Bear Island

Fool's gold
Frobisher and his crew found glistening rocks, but they turned out to be worthless pyrite, or "fool's gold."

Icebergs

Sailing for Spain
Although born in the Italian port of Genoa, Columbus was sponsored by Queen Isabella of Spain.

Great Bear Lake

Great Slave Lake

Lake Winnipeg

Great Lakes

NORTH AMERICA

Rockies

Making repairs
Before setting off across the Indian Ocean, Drake landed to repair his ship, the *Golden Hind*, close to present-day San Francisco. He claimed the region for England.

Pacific Ocean

Easy fishing
The Grand Banks off Newfoundland were so rich in cod that Cabot's crew could simply scoop them out of the sea with baskets.

AMSTERDAM
Bristol
LONDON
Plymouth
EUROP

MADRID
LISBON
Palos Seville

Atlantic Ocean

Fort in Elmina
This fort was built by the Portuguese in 1482 to protect their gold trade from the Spanish.

ELMINA
AFRICA

Congo

See inset (below)

Guatulco

Seeking treasure
Drake attacked and captured a Spanish treasure ship off the coast of Peru, returning to England as a very rich man.

The first fleet
Columbus had three ships on his first voyage: the *Niña*, the *Pinta*, and the *Santa Maria*.

Columbus landing in San Salvador, in the Bahamas, on his first voyage to the New World

Amazon

SOUTH AMERICA

Andes

Stone guides
Like his fellow Portuguese navigators before him, Dias erected a stone *padrao* (pillar) to mark the farthest point of his voyage and to guide future sailors.

Arawak native

San Salvador

CUBA

La Navidad **HISPANIOLA**

Columbus founding the settlement of La Navidad during his first voyage

| 0 | 500km |
| 0 | 250 miles |

Alligator in Panama

Columbus reaching the Americas

Storms around Cape Horn, on the southern tip of South America

Dias sailing around the southern tip of Africa

Southern Ocean

Navigation

The first European explorers had few instruments to help them and often sailed in the wrong direction. They did, however, use a magnetic compass (left) to follow a set course. To figure out their latitude (how far north or south they were) they used an astrolabe to measure the height of the Sun at noon and a quadrant or a cross-staff, both of which measured the height of a star. Navigators had no way of calculating their longitude (how far east or west they were) until the invention of the marine chronometer in 1759.

Ice-bound
In his search for the Northeast Passage to Asia, Barents's ship got stuck in the ice. He and his crew had to spend the winter of 1596 in a hut that they built on the shore.

Arctic Ocean

0 — 4,000km
0 — 2,000 miles

Ural Mountains

ASIA

Vasco da Gama in India
Da Gama reached India in 1498 and met the Hindu ruler of Calicut. He had little to exchange with the rich ruler and returned home with only a few spices.

Lake Baikal

Aral Sea

Caspian Sea

Himalayas

Yellow river

Chang Jiang

CALICUT

Lake Victoria

Arab traders
Arab merchants controlled trade in the western Indian Ocean, shipping goods to and from the Persian Gulf, India, and Africa.

MOMBASA
Arab sailing ships

Across the ocean
Magellan took four months to cross the Pacific Ocean, sighting a few uninhabited islands before landing in Guam in March 1521.

PHILIPPINES

Pacific Ocean

Guam

Cebu

EAST INDIES

Death of Magellan
Magellan never completed his around-the-world voyage. He was killed in a skirmish on the island of Cebu, in the Philippines, in 1521.

Spice Islands

Food of the Spice Islands (Moluccas), in the East Indies

Indian Ocean

AUSTRALIA

oa Bay

Unwelcome visitor
Da Gama visited the busy trading port of Mombasa, but he fled when the local Muslim ruler attacked his two ships.

Lonely voyage home
Magellan began his voyage with five ships and a large crew. After his death, Sebastián de Elcano battled through storms to return home to Spain in 1522, with only one ship and 17 crew.

Southern Ocean

1450

1460 Death of Prince Henry "the Navigator," the first Portuguese sponsor (financial supporter) of voyages of discovery

1485–1486 Diogo Cao sails down the west African coast for Portugal
1487–1488 Dias becomes the first European to sail around the southern tip of Africa into the Indian Ocean
1492–1493 Columbus becomes the first European to sail to the Americas
1493–1496 Columbus's second voyage, to the West Indies
1494 Treaty of Tordesillas divides the undiscovered world between Portugal and Spain
1497 Italian John Cabot sails to Newfoundland for the English king
1497–1498 Vasco da Gama opens up a new trade route from Europe across the Indian Ocean to India
1498–1500 Columbus's third voyage: he becomes the first European to land in South America

1500

1502–1504 Columbus's fourth voyage: he lands in Central America

1519–1521 Magellan becomes the first European to sail across the Pacific Ocean
1521–1522 Sebastián de Elcano completes Magellan's voyage as the first person to sail around the world

1527–1528 Pánfilo de Narváez explores the Gulf of Mexico for Spain

1534 Jacques Cartier searches for a Northwest Passage to Asia for the French king, but he discovers Canada instead

1550

1567–1569 Álvaro de Mendaña explores the southern Pacific Ocean for Spain

1576 Martin Frobisher explores the Northwest Passage for England
1577–1580 Francis Drake sails around the world

1596–1598 Dutch navigator Willem Barents explores the Northeast Passage

1600

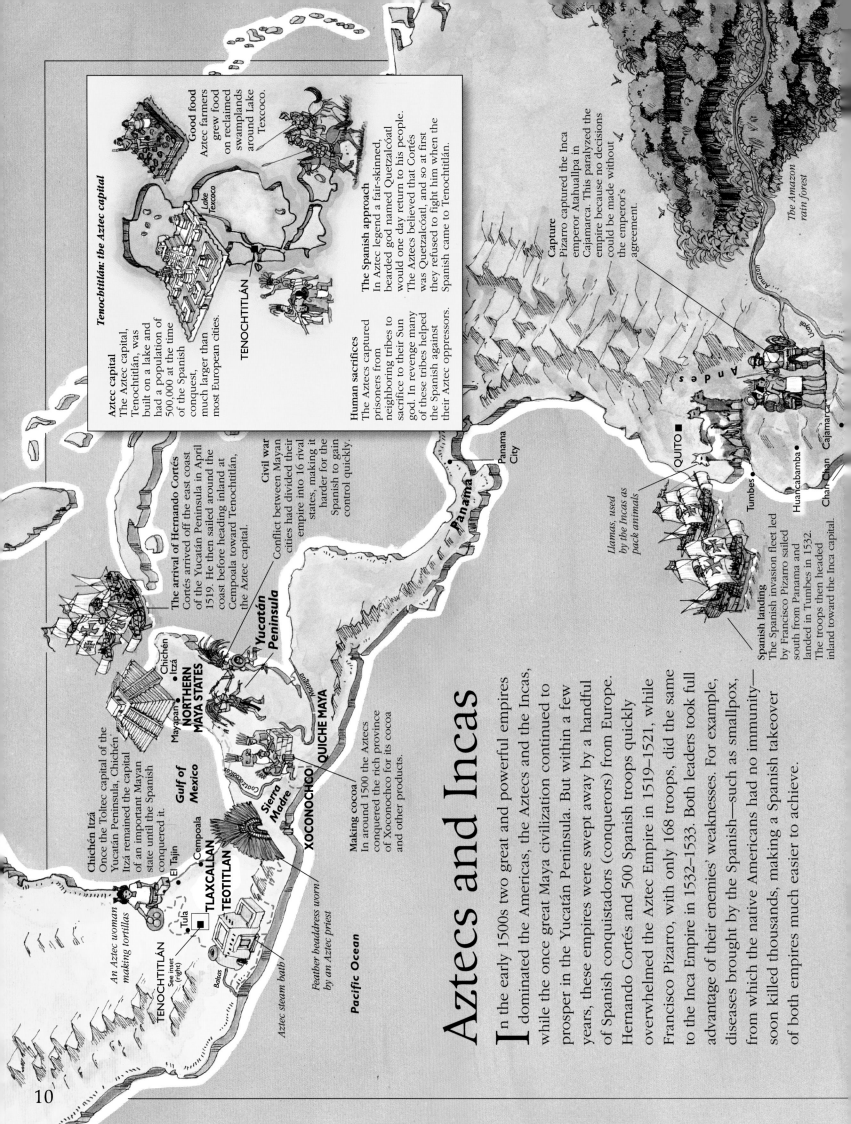

Aztecs and Incas

In the early 1500s two great and powerful empires dominated the Americas, the Aztecs and the Incas, while the once great Maya civilization continued to prosper in the Yucatán Peninsula. But within a few years, these empires were swept away by a handful of Spanish conquistadors (conquerors) from Europe. Hernando Cortés and 500 Spanish troops quickly overwhelmed the Aztec Empire in 1519–1521, while Francisco Pizarro, with only 168 troops, did the same to the Inca Empire in 1532–1533. Both leaders took full advantage of their enemies' weaknesses. For example, diseases brought by the Spanish—such as smallpox, from which the native Americans had no immunity—soon killed thousands, making a Spanish takeover of both empires much easier to achieve.

Tenochtitlán: the Aztec capital

Aztec capital
The Aztec capital, Tenochtitlán, was built on a lake and had a population of 500,000 at the time of the Spanish conquest, much larger than most European cities.

Human sacrifices
The Aztecs captured prisoners from neighboring tribes to sacrifice to their Sun god. In revenge many of these tribes helped the Spanish against their Aztec oppressors.

The Spanish approach
In Aztec legend a fair-skinned, bearded god named Quetzalcóatl would one day return to his people. The Aztecs believed that Cortés was Quetzalcóatl, and so at first they refused to fight him when the Spanish came to Tenochtitlán.

Good food
Aztec farmers grew food on reclaimed swamplands around Lake Texcoco.

Lake Texcoco

TENOCHTITLÁN

Chichén Itzá
Once the Toltec capital of the Yucatán Peninsula, Chichén Itzá remained the capital of an important Mayan state until the Spanish conquered it.

The arrival of Hernando Cortés
Cortés arrived off the east coast of the Yucatán Peninsula in April 1519. He then sailed around the coast before heading inland at Cempoala toward Tenochtitlán, the Aztec capital.

Civil war
Conflict between Mayan cities had divided their empire into 16 rival states, making it harder for the Spanish to gain control quickly.

Making cocoa
In around 1500 the Aztecs conquered the rich province of Xoconochco for its cocoa and other products.

An Aztec woman making tortillas

TENOCHTITLÁN
See inset (right)

Tula
TLAXCALLAN
TEOTITLAN
El Tajín
Cempoala

Gulf of Mexico

Feather headdress worn by an Aztec priest

Pacific Ocean

Aztec steam bath

Bolsas

Sierra Madre

Coatzacoalcos

XOCONOCHCO

QUICHE MAYA

Yucatán Peninsula

Chichén Itzá
Mayapan
NORTHERN MAYA STATES

Panama
Panama City

Llamas, used by the Incas as pack animals

QUITO

Capture
Pizarro captured the Inca emperor Atahuallpa in Cajamarca. This paralyzed the empire because no decisions could be made without the emperor's agreement.

Spanish landing
The Spanish invasion fleet led by Francisco Pizarro sailed south from Panama and landed in Tumbes in 1532. The troops then headed inland toward the Inca capital.

Tumbes
Huancabamba
Chan Chan
Cajamarca

Andes

Amazon

The Amazon rain forest

Protecting the capital
The stone fortress of Sacsahuaman protected Cuzco. It was large enough for every person in the city to retreat within its walls during times of crisis.

Growing potatoes

Keeping records
The Incas recorded information about their population, taxes, harvests, and other items on knotted strings known as *quipos*.

Growing maize in the valleys

• Huánco
• Jauja
Machu Picchu ■ CUZCO
Vilcas •
Vitcos •

Reed boat on Lake Titicaca
Lake Titicaca

• Pica
• Cartarpe
Building a stone road
Pucara de Andalgala •
• Copiapo
• Ranchillos
• Santiago
• Talca

Inca capital
The Incas considered their capital city to be the center of the universe. In their Quechua language the word *cuzco* means "navel" (belly).

Terraced farms
The Incas made terraces in the mountainsides to farm crops because their empire contained few flat valleys in which to grow food.

Fishing
Inshore fishing provided the Incas with most of their protein.

---- this dotted line shows the extent of the Aztec Empire in 1520

---- this dotted line shows the extent of the Maya Empire in 1520

---- this dotted line shows the extent of the Inca Empire in 1525

Pacific Ocean

1,000km
500 miles
0 0

The Spanish conquest

Although small in number, the Spanish were able to conquer the mighty Aztec, Maya, and Inca empires because they were much better armed and fought on horses, which were unknown in the Americas at that time. Most importantly, the Spanish were able to exploit their enemies' weaknesses: many local tribes hated the bloodthirsty Aztecs and fought with the Spanish against them, while the Inca Empire had not yet recovered from a lengthy civil war. Only the Mayas held out for a long period because they were divided into 16 different city-states, making it difficult for the Spanish to conquer them all at one time. This picture (above) shows native Americans receiving Christian communion from a Spanish priest.

ycmoquayatcq
que tlatoque

1450

1450 Pachacutec, Inca emperor since 1438, massively expands the empire

1470 Incas conquer Chimu Empire
1471–1493 Tupac Yupanqui expands the Inca Empire south

1475

1480 Civil war breaks out in Maya Empire

1494–1525 Inca Empire reaches its largest size under Huayna Capac

1500

1502–1520 Aztec Empire reaches its largest size under Montezuma II

1519–1521 Cortés invades the Aztec Empire
1520 Montezuma II killed by the Spanish
1521 Spanish take Tenochtitlán
1524 Spanish begin to conquer the Mayan city-states

1525

1525–1532 Civil war in Inca Empire between the sons of Huayna Capac

1532 Pizarro invades Inca Empire and captures Emperor Atahuallpa
1533 Spanish execute Atahuallpa and install a "puppet" emperor, Thupu Wallpa, who they can control

1536 Spanish take direct control of the Inca Empire

1550

1572 Last Inca resistance crushed in the mountain strongholds

1575

1600 Mayan resistance to the Spanish continues until 1697

1600

Charles V and the Hapsburg Empire
Charles V of Spain was the master of Europe. Born in 1500, he inherited the Rhineland and the Netherlands from his Hapsburg father, plus Spain and its Italian and American empires from his Spanish grandfather and mother. In 1519 he inherited Hapsburg Austria from his grandfather and was elected the Holy Roman Emperor, effectively, the ruler of Germany. He abdicated (resigned) in 1556 and died in 1558.

School of Navigation
In 1416 Prince Henry, "the Navigator," the son of the king of Portugal, opened a navigation school in Sagres to promote exploration and discovery.

Spain and its empire

In the early 1500s Spain, ruled by the Hapsburg family of Austria, emerged as the most powerful nation in Europe. The country and its king, Charles V, had gained a large European empire through marriage and inheritance, and then a second empire in the Americas through conquest. Spain became the major Catholic power in Europe and led the fight against the Protestant Reformation (see pages 16–17). Spanish power attracted many enemies, and the empire soon proved to be too big for one person to rule. In 1556 Charles V split his empire in two, giving Spain and its territories to his son and other lands to his brother.

The Spanish Armada
In 1588 a large fleet left La Coruña to invade England and depose the Protestant queen, Elizabeth I. The fleet was defeated by a combination of the English navy and very bad weather.

Don Quixote
The Spanish writer Miguel de Cervantes wrote the classic story of *Don Quixote*. It was published in two parts, in 1605 and 1615.

The Escorial Pala
Philip II ordered huge palace to be bu outside of Madrid, fro which to govern h huge Europe and America empi

Taking over Portugal
In 1580 Philip II of Spain defeated the Portuguese in Alcantara and seized the Portuguese throne. Spain held on to Portugal's huge empire until 1640.

The Morisco revolt
Islamic Moors were converted to Christianity by force in 1492. They rebelled against Spanish rule 70 years later.

Joint monarchs
In 1469 Ferdinand of Aragon married Isabella of Castile. In 1479 they both succeeded to their thrones and ruled their countries jointly, uniting Spain.

The end of Moorish rule
Ferdinand and Isabella finally drove the Moors out of Granada in 1492, ending 781 years of Muslim rule in Spain.

Raiding parties
English privateers (pirates sent by the government) led by Francis Drake regularly raided Spanish ports to seize American treasures and disrupt shipping.

Coastal forts
The Spaniards built a series of forts along the north African coast, from which to control the western Mediterranean and fight the Ottomans.

Heading south
After 1432 Portuguese navigators began to explore the west coast of Africa, setting up trading posts as they sailed farther south.

La Coruña

PORTUGAL

Cork tree

Douro

Ebro

MADRID ■

SPAIN

Castile

• Toledo

Tagus

• Alcantara

LISBON

Guadiana

Toledo cathedral

Córdoba •

Guadalquivir

Seville •

Granada

Atlantic Ocean

• Cadiz

• Ceuta

Tangier •

• Melilla

North Africa

Sagres •

0   200km
0   100 miles

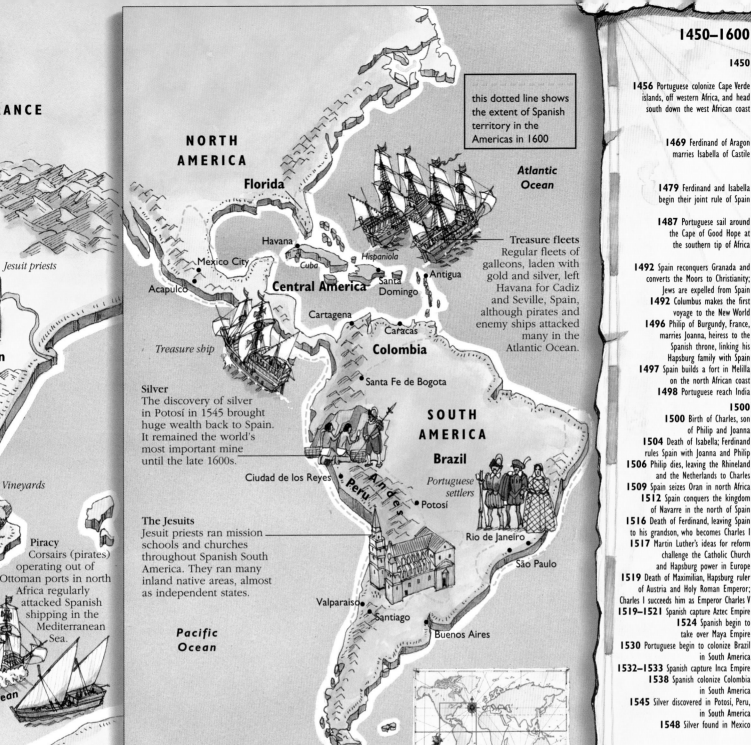

FRANCE

Navarre

Jesuit priests

Aragon

Vineyards

Piracy
Corsairs (pirates) operating out of Ottoman ports in north Africa regularly attacked Spanish shipping in the Mediterranean Sea.

Mediterranean Sea

• Oran

NORTH AMERICA

Florida

Havana

Mexico City

Cuba

Hispaniola

Acapulco

Central America

Santa Domingo

• Antigua

Cartagena

Caracas

Treasure ship

Colombia

Santa Fe de Bogota

Silver
The discovery of silver in Potosí in 1545 brought huge wealth back to Spain. It remained the world's most important mine until the late 1600s.

SOUTH AMERICA

Brazil

Portuguese settlers

Ciudad de los Reyes

Andes

Peru

• Potosí

Rio de Janeiro

The Jesuits
Jesuit priests ran mission schools and churches throughout Spanish South America. They ran many inland native areas, almost as independent states.

São Paulo

Pacific Ocean

Valparaiso

Santiago

Buenos Aires

Atlantic Ocean

this dotted line shows the extent of Spanish territory in the Americas in 1600

Treasure fleets
Regular fleets of galleons, laden with gold and silver, left Havana for Cadiz and Seville, Spain, although pirates and enemy ships attacked many in the Atlantic Ocean.

0   3,000km

0   1,500 miles

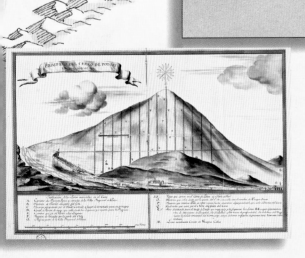

Spanish wealth

The gold and silver mines in Mexico and Peru brought incredible wealth to Spain. Large galleons, accompanied by armed warships, carried the bullion across the Atlantic Ocean. Despite these precautions, pirates and enemy ships, especially from England and Holland, often attacked the fleets. This wealth enabled Spain to dominate Europe because it could afford to pay for large armies, but it also caused prices to rise at home, eventually ruining the Spanish economy. This picture shows a plan of the silver mines in Potosí, in modern-day Bolivia.

1456 Portuguese colonize Cape Verde islands, off western Africa, and head south down the west African coast

1469 Ferdinand of Aragon marries Isabella of Castile

1479 Ferdinand and Isabella begin their joint rule of Spain

1487 Portuguese sail around the Cape of Good Hope at the southern tip of Africa

1492 Spain reconquers Granada and converts the Moors to Christianity; Jews are expelled from Spain
1492 Columbus makes the first voyage to the New World
1496 Philip of Burgundy, France, marries Joanna, heiress to the Spanish throne, linking his Hapsburg family with Spain
1497 Spain builds a fort in Melilla on the north African coast
1498 Portuguese reach India

1500

1500 Birth of Charles, son of Philip and Joanna
1504 Death of Isabella; Ferdinand rules Spain with Joanna and Philip
1506 Philip dies, leaving the Rhineland and the Netherlands to Charles
1509 Spain seizes Oran in north Africa
1512 Spain conquers the kingdom of Navarre in the north of Spain
1516 Death of Ferdinand, leaving Spain to his grandson, who becomes Charles I
1517 Martin Luther's ideas for reform challenge the Catholic Church and Hapsburg power in Europe
1519 Death of Maximilian, Hapsburg ruler of Austria and Holy Roman Emperor; Charles I succeeds him as Emperor Charles V
1519–1521 Spanish capture Aztec Empire
1524 Spanish begin to take over Maya Empire
1530 Portuguese begin to colonize Brazil in South America
1532–1533 Spanish capture Inca Empire
1538 Spanish colonize Colombia in South America
1545 Silver discovered in Potosí, Peru, in South America
1548 Silver found in Mexico

1550

1556 Charles V abdicates; Philip II succeeds him in Spain; Charles's brother Ferdinand becomes the Holy Roman Emperor

1563–1584 Escorial Palace is built by the order of Philip II
1565 Spanish colonize Florida, in North America, and build a fort there to protect their gold bullion fleets
1566 Dutch begin a revolt against Spanish rule
1569–1571 Moriscos revolt in southern Spain
1571 Spanish begin to colonize the Philippines; Manila is founded
1574 Spanish lose the important port of Tunis to the Ottomans

1580–1640 Spain rules Portugal and its empire
1581 Spain makes peace with the Ottomans

1588 Spanish Armada fails to invade England

1598 Philip II dies; Philip III succeeds him

1600

The Renaissance:
A world of new learning

The Renaissance—a French word meaning "rebirth"—was an artistic, cultural, and intellectual movement that influenced all of the arts and sciences. Renaissance artists and scholars looked back to the art and education of classical Rome and Greece for their inspiration, reviving the past in order to develop and explore new ideas and methods. This new approach became known as "humanism," because it encouraged people to achieve things for themselves, rather than simply to accept what they were taught to be true. The Renaissance began in Italy during the 1300s and reached its height during the 1400s and 1500s, spreading across all of western and northern Europe.

Scientific invention
A "Renaissance man" or "universal man" was someone who could do many things. One such person was Leonardo da Vinci (1452–1519), who, as well as being an artist and a sculptor, drew plans for a helicopter (above), a flying machine, and a tank. He also dissected human bodies to find out more about how we move and function.

Renaissance art
Renaissance artists depicted people and landscapes in a very natural way, studying anatomy and perspective to make their paintings look more realistic. Michelangelo (1475–1564) was perhaps the greatest Renaissance artist, creating lifelike sculptures, such as his *David* (left), and huge paintings such as the ceiling of the Sistine Chapel in Rome, Italy.

Astronomy
The Renaissance encouraged scientists to explore new ideas and to challenge existing beliefs. In 1543 the Polish astronomer Nicolaus Copernicus (1473–1543) proposed that the Sun was at the center of the solar system and that all of the planets revolved around it. This shocked many people, because their religious teachings had always insisted that Earth was at the center of the universe. The chart above shows the arrangement that was suggested by Copernicus.

14

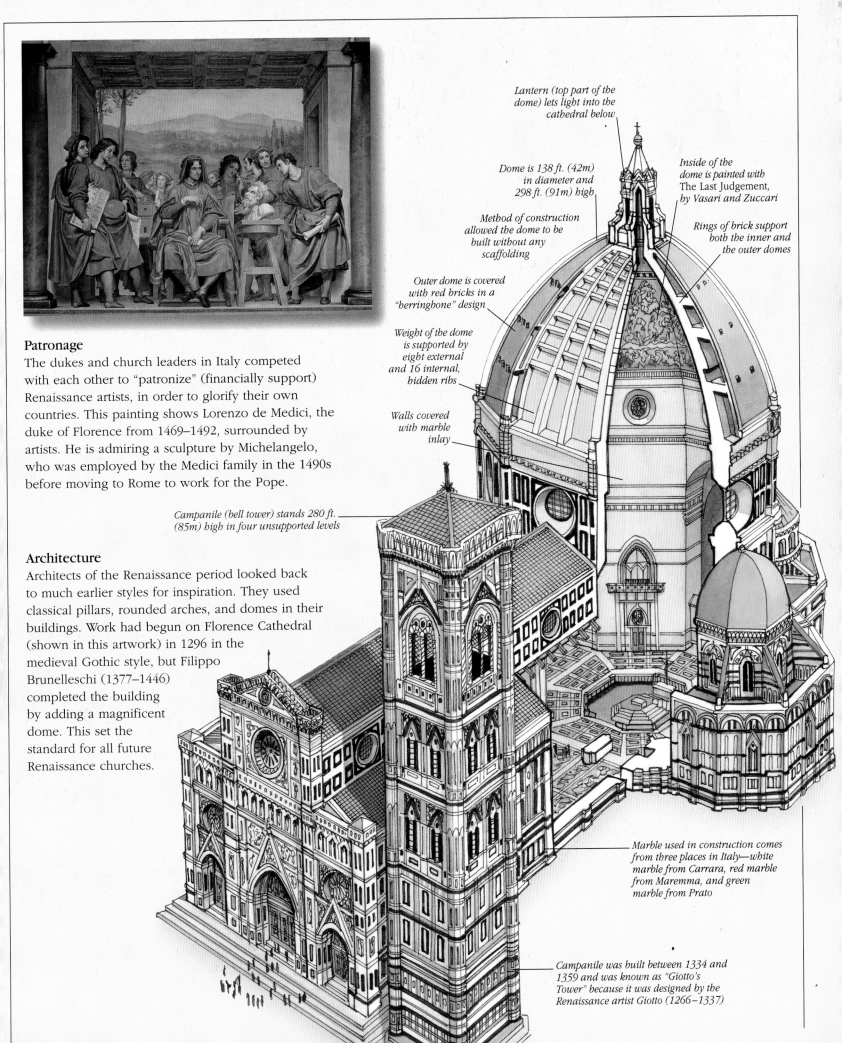

Patronage

The dukes and church leaders in Italy competed with each other to "patronize" (financially support) Renaissance artists, in order to glorify their own countries. This painting shows Lorenzo de Medici, the duke of Florence from 1469–1492, surrounded by artists. He is admiring a sculpture by Michelangelo, who was employed by the Medici family in the 1490s before moving to Rome to work for the Pope.

Architecture

Architects of the Renaissance period looked back to much earlier styles for inspiration. They used classical pillars, rounded arches, and domes in their buildings. Work had begun on Florence Cathedral (shown in this artwork) in 1296 in the medieval Gothic style, but Filippo Brunelleschi (1377–1446) completed the building by adding a magnificent dome. This set the standard for all future Renaissance churches.

Lantern (top part of the dome) lets light into the cathedral below

Dome is 138 ft. (42m) in diameter and 298 ft. (91m) high

Method of construction allowed the dome to be built without any scaffolding

Inside of the dome is painted with The Last Judgement, by Vasari and Zuccari

Rings of brick support both the inner and the outer domes

Outer dome is covered with red bricks in a "herringbone" design

Weight of the dome is supported by eight external and 16 internal, hidden ribs

Walls covered with marble inlay

Campanile (bell tower) stands 280 ft. (85m) high in four unsupported levels

Marble used in construction comes from three places in Italy—white marble from Carrara, red marble from Maremma, and green marble from Prato

Campanile was built between 1334 and 1359 and was known as "Giotto's Tower" because it was designed by the Renaissance artist Giotto (1266–1337)

15

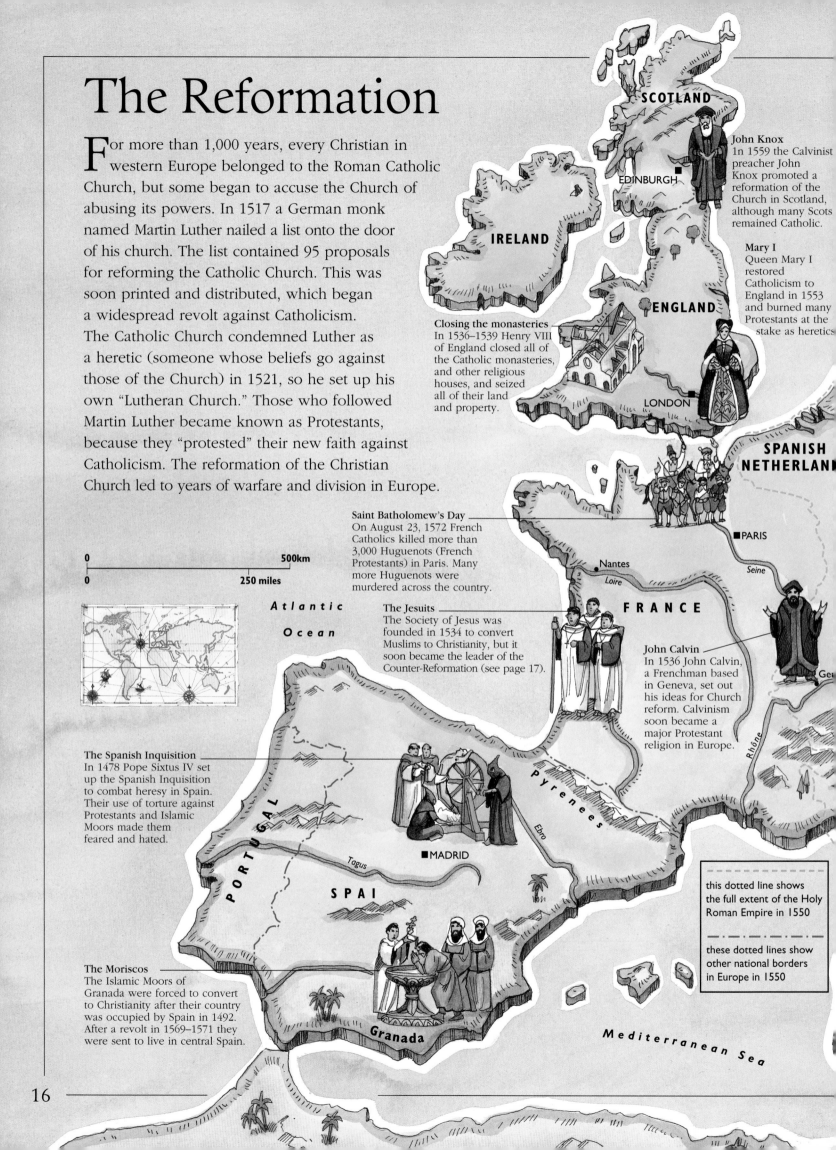

The Reformation

For more than 1,000 years, every Christian in western Europe belonged to the Roman Catholic Church, but some began to accuse the Church of abusing its powers. In 1517 a German monk named Martin Luther nailed a list onto the door of his church. The list contained 95 proposals for reforming the Catholic Church. This was soon printed and distributed, which began a widespread revolt against Catholicism. The Catholic Church condemned Luther as a heretic (someone whose beliefs go against those of the Church) in 1521, so he set up his own "Lutheran Church." Those who followed Martin Luther became known as Protestants, because they "protested" their new faith against Catholicism. The reformation of the Christian Church led to years of warfare and division in Europe.

SCOTLAND

EDINBURGH

IRELAND

John Knox
In 1559 the Calvinist preacher John Knox promoted a reformation of the Church in Scotland, although many Scots remained Catholic.

Mary I
Queen Mary I restored Catholicism to England in 1553 and burned many Protestants at the stake as heretics

ENGLAND

Closing the monasteries
In 1536–1539 Henry VIII of England closed all of the Catholic monasteries, and other religious houses, and seized all of their land and property.

LONDON

SPANISH NETHERLAND

0   500km
0   250 miles

Atlantic Ocean

Saint Batholomew's Day
On August 23, 1572 French Catholics killed more than 3,000 Huguenots (French Protestants) in Paris. Many more Huguenots were murdered across the country.

■ PARIS

Seine

Nantes

Loire

The Jesuits
The Society of Jesus was founded in 1534 to convert Muslims to Christianity, but it soon became the leader of the Counter-Reformation (see page 17).

FRANCE

John Calvin
In 1536 John Calvin, a Frenchman based in Geneva, set out his ideas for Church reform. Calvinism soon became a major Protestant religion in Europe.

Ger

The Spanish Inquisition
In 1478 Pope Sixtus IV set up the Spanish Inquisition to combat heresy in Spain. Their use of torture against Protestants and Islamic Moors made them feared and hated.

Pyrenees

Ebro

Rhône

P O R T U G A L

Tagus

■ MADRID

S P A I

The Moriscos
The Islamic Moors of Granada were forced to convert to Christianity after their country was occupied by Spain in 1492. After a revolt in 1569–1571 they were sent to live in central Spain.

Granada

Mediterranean Sea

this dotted line shows the full extent of the Holy Roman Empire in 1550

these dotted lines show other national borders in Europe in 1550

Martin Luther

Martin Luther (1483–1546), pictured here in dark robes, was an Augustinian friar and professor of theology at Wittenberg University in Saxony. He objected to many aspects of Catholic beliefs and practices, but he at first wanted to reform the Church, not divide it. When this proved to be impossible, he set up his own reformed Church.

North Sea

Baltic Sea

NORWAY

DENMARK

SWEDEN

Gutenberg's printing press, developed in the 1440s

Radical preachers

German Catholic church in flames

Elbe

Wittenberg

Saxony

Germany

Worms

HOLY ROMAN EMPIRE

Rhine

SWISS CONFEDERATION

Bavaria

Danube

Augsburg

Zürich

Corpernicus
In 1531 Copernicus, a Polish astronomer, demonstrated that the planets move around the Sun, and not around Earth. This went against the teachings of the Catholic Church.

The 95 Theses
In 1517 Martin Luther nailed 95 proposals for Catholic reform to the door of his church in Wittenberg, Saxony.

POLAND

Expelling Protestants
In the late 1550s Protestants were thrown out of Bavaria and Austria as the Catholic Church regained its control. Poland had also become Catholic again.

Council of Trent
Catholic officials met in Trent three times after 1545.

Austria

Trent

P S

Po

VENICE

HUNGARY

OTTOMAN EMPIRE

PAPAL STATES

■ROME

Saint Peter's Basilica in Rome, Italy

The Counter-Reformation

From 1545 to 1563, the Roman Catholic Church met in Trent, in the Italian Alps, to reform the Church and to help it fight back against Protestantism. The Counter-Reformation saw great changes in practice, and religious buildings in the new Baroque style of architecture—such as Saint Peter's Basilica in Rome, Italy (above)—helped attract people back into the Catholic Church.

The Pope
As a result of the Reformation, Rome's role as the headquarters of the Christian Church was reduced, but the Pope remained an important figure in Europe for many years.

1510–1600

1510

1517 Martin Luther nails 95 proposals for Catholic reform to the door of his church in Wittenberg, Saxony

1520

1521 Luther presents his ideas for reform to the Holy Roman Emperor at the Diet (council) of Worms
1523 In Zürich Ulrich Zwingli proposes 67 reforms to the Catholic Church
1524 Religious warfare breaks out in Germany as peasants rise up in revolt
1525 Lutheranism is the state religion of Saxony and many other German states

1530

1531 Copernicus suggests the Sun, not Earth, is at the center of the universe
1534 Society of Jesus (Jesuits) forms
1534 Henry VIII of England breaks away from the Catholic Church when it refuses to grant him a divorce
1536 John Calvin sets out his ideas for religious reforms in his book, *Institutes*
1536–1539 Henry VIII closes monasteries

1540

1541 John Calvin begins to organize a strict Protestant Church in Geneva

1544 Sweden converts to Lutheranism
1545–1563 The Roman Catholic Church meets three times in Trent, in the Alps, to launch the Counter-Reformation against Protestant Churches

1550

1553–1558 England briefly becomes Catholic again under Mary I
1555 After years of war Holy Roman Emperor agrees the Peace of Augsburg, giving each ruler within the empire the right to choose their own state religion
1558 Elizabeth I comes to the throne and restores Protestantism to England

1560

1560 Scottish Parliament declares Scotland to be a Protestant nation
1562–1580 French wars of religion divide the country

1566 Dutch Protestants rise up in revolt against Spanish Catholic rulers

1570

1572 Thousands of French Huguenots (Protestants) are massacred by Catholics

1580

1589 The Huguenot Henry Navarre becomes Henry IV of France
1590

1593 Henry IV of France becomes a Catholic

1598 Edict of Nantes grants religious tolerance to Huguenots in France

1600

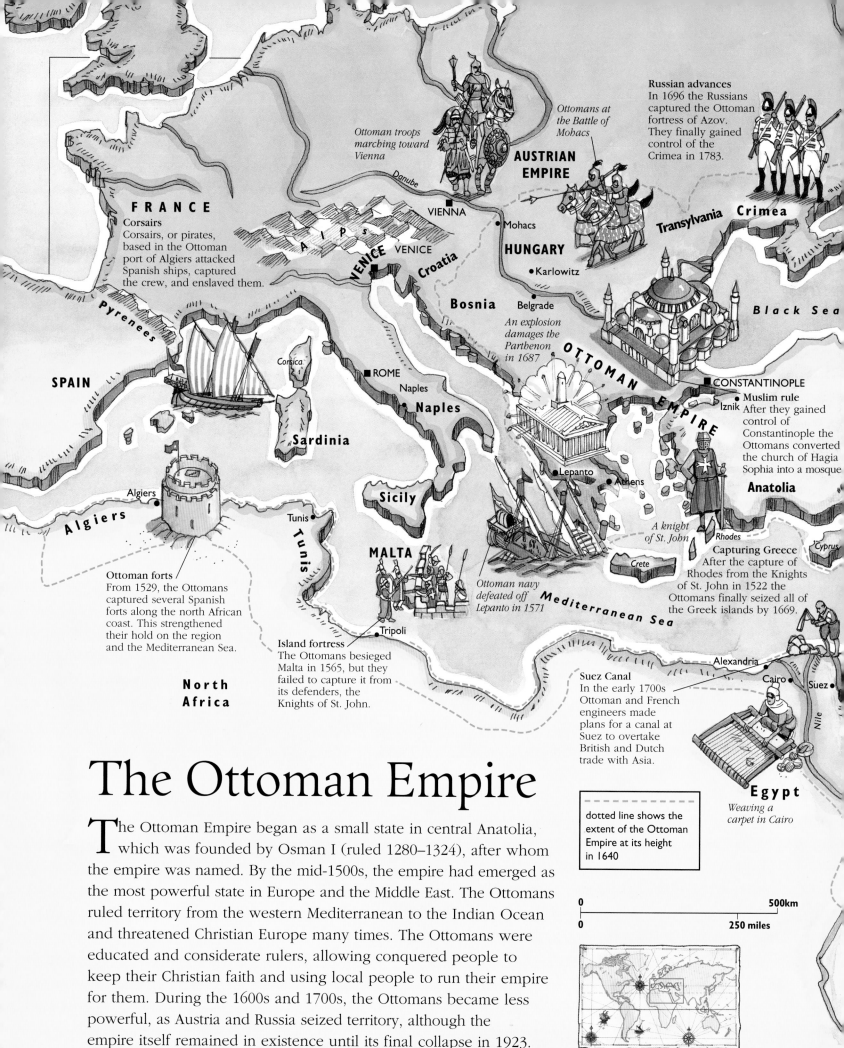

FRANCE

Corsairs
Corsairs, or pirates, based in the Ottoman port of Algiers attacked Spanish ships, captured the crew, and enslaved them.

Ottoman troops marching toward Vienna

Ottomans at the Battle of Mohacs

AUSTRIAN EMPIRE

Russian advances
In 1696 the Russians captured the Ottoman fortress of Azov. They finally gained control of the Crimea in 1783.

Transylvania   **Crimea**

VIENNA

Mohacs

HUNGARY

Karlowitz

Croatia

VENICE   VENICE

Bosnia

Belgrade

An explosion damages the Parthenon in 1687

Black Sea

Pyrenees

SPAIN

Corsica

■ ROME

Naples

Naples

Sardinia

CONSTANTINOPLE

■ **Muslim rule**
Iznik   After they gained control of Constantinople the Ottomans converted the church of Hagia Sophia into a mosque

Anatolia

Lepanto

Athens

A knight of St. John

Rhodes

Capturing Greece
After the capture of Rhodes from the Knights of St. John in 1522 the Ottomans finally seized all of the Greek islands by 1669.

Cyprus

Algiers

Algiers

Ottoman forts
From 1529, the Ottomans captured several Spanish forts along the north African coast. This strengthened their hold on the region and the Mediterranean Sea.

North Africa

Sicily

Tunis

Tunis

MALTA

Tripoli

Island fortress
The Ottomans besieged Malta in 1565, but they failed to capture it from its defenders, the Knights of St. John.

Crete

Ottoman navy defeated off Lepanto in 1571

Mediterranean Sea

Alexandria

Cairo   Suez

Suez Canal
In the early 1700s Ottoman and French engineers made plans for a canal at Suez to overtake British and Dutch trade with Asia.

Nile

Egypt
Weaving a carpet in Cairo

The Ottoman Empire

The Ottoman Empire began as a small state in central Anatolia, which was founded by Osman I (ruled 1280–1324), after whom the empire was named. By the mid-1500s, the empire had emerged as the most powerful state in Europe and the Middle East. The Ottomans ruled territory from the western Mediterranean to the Indian Ocean and threatened Christian Europe many times. The Ottomans were educated and considerate rulers, allowing conquered people to keep their Christian faith and using local people to run their empire for them. During the 1600s and 1700s, the Ottomans became less powerful, as Austria and Russia seized territory, although the empire itself remained in existence until its final collapse in 1923.

dotted line shows the extent of the Ottoman Empire at its height in 1640

0   500km

0   250 miles

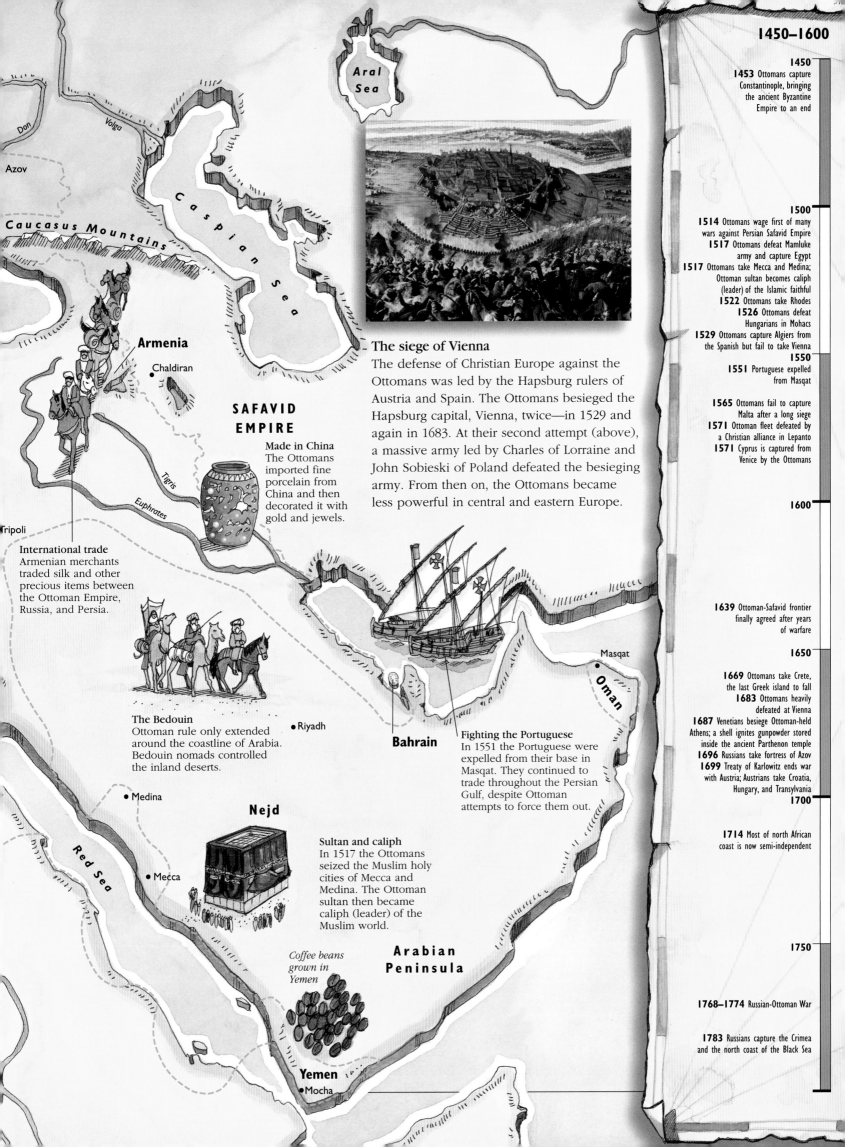

Don

Volga

Azov

Caucasus Mountains

Caspian Sea

Armenia

Chaldiran

SAFAVID EMPIRE

Tigris

Euphrates

Tripoli

Aral Sea

Made in China
The Ottomans imported fine porcelain from China and then decorated it with gold and jewels.

The siege of Vienna
The defense of Christian Europe against the Ottomans was led by the Hapsburg rulers of Austria and Spain. The Ottomans besieged the Hapsburg capital, Vienna, twice—in 1529 and again in 1683. At their second attempt (above), a massive army led by Charles of Lorraine and John Sobieski of Poland defeated the besieging army. From then on, the Ottomans became less powerful in central and eastern Europe.

International trade
Armenian merchants traded silk and other precious items between the Ottoman Empire, Russia, and Persia.

The Bedouin
Ottoman rule only extended around the coastline of Arabia. Bedouin nomads controlled the inland deserts.

• Riyadh

Masqat

Oman

Bahrain

Fighting the Portuguese
In 1551 the Portuguese were expelled from their base in Masqat. They continued to trade throughout the Persian Gulf, despite Ottoman attempts to force them out.

• Medina

Nejd

Sultan and caliph
In 1517 the Ottomans seized the Muslim holy cities of Mecca and Medina. The Ottoman sultan then became caliph (leader) of the Muslim world.

Red Sea

• Mecca

Coffee beans grown in Yemen

Arabian Peninsula

Yemen

•Mocha

1450–1600

1450

1453 Ottomans capture Constantinople, bringing the ancient Byzantine Empire to an end

1500

1514 Ottomans wage first of many wars against Persian Safavid Empire
1517 Ottomans defeat Mamluke army and capture Egypt
1517 Ottomans take Mecca and Medina; Ottoman sultan becomes caliph (leader) of the Islamic faithful
1522 Ottomans take Rhodes
1526 Ottomans defeat Hungarians in Mohacs
1529 Ottomans capture Algiers from the Spanish but fail to take Vienna

1550

1551 Portuguese expelled from Masqat

1565 Ottomans fail to capture Malta after a long siege
1571 Ottoman fleet defeated by a Christian alliance in Lepanto
1571 Cyprus is captured from Venice by the Ottomans

1600

1639 Ottoman-Safavid frontier finally agreed after years of warfare

1650

1669 Ottomans take Crete, the last Greek island to fall
1683 Ottomans heavily defeated at Vienna
1687 Venetians besiege Ottoman-held Athens; a shell ignites gunpowder stored inside the ancient Parthenon temple
1696 Russians take fortress of Azov
1699 Treaty of Karlowitz ends war with Austria; Austrians take Croatia, Hungary, and Transylvania

1700

1714 Most of north African coast is now semi-independent

1750

1768–1774 Russian-Ottoman War

1783 Russians capture the Crimea and the north coast of the Black Sea

The Mogul Empire

In the late 1400s the Moguls—descendants of the famous Mongol leader Timur—were driven out of central Asia by the Mongol Tatars. They moved south and began to raid India, mounting a full-scale invasion in 1526. They soon conquered northern India, and by 1600, they were advancing south into the Deccan. One hundred years later they controlled everything except the far south. The Moguls were good administrators; although Muslim, they allowed their Hindu and Sikh subjects to worship freely. In the 1700s the Mogul Empire came under attack from the Hindu Marathas of the west coast, while the French and British also gained territory. By 1800, the British had defeated the French and dominated Mogul India.

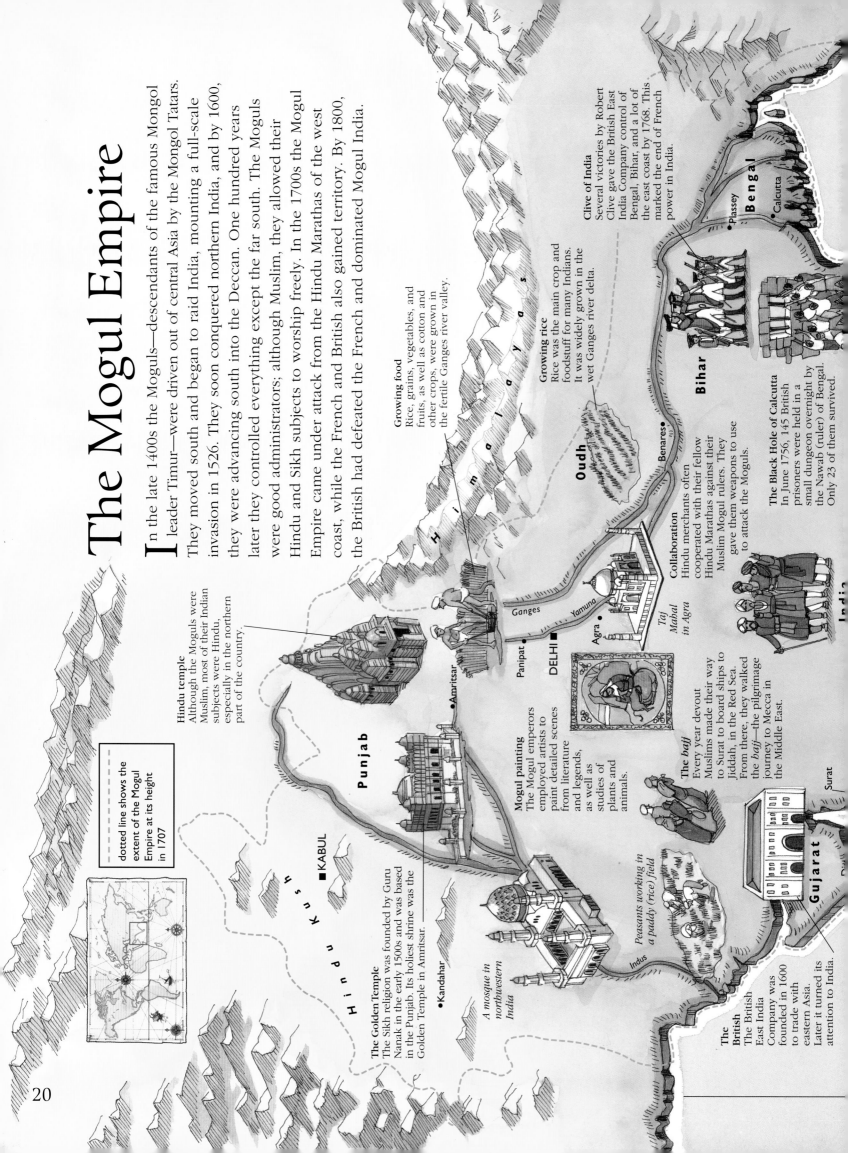

dotted line shows the extent of the Mogul Empire at its height in 1707

Hindu temple
Although the Moguls were Muslim, most of their Indian subjects were Hindu, especially in the northern part of the country.

The Golden Temple
The Sikh religion was founded by Guru Nanak in the early 1500s and was based in the Punjab. Its holiest shrine was the Golden Temple in Amritsar.

Mogul painting
The Mogul emperors employed artists to paint detailed scenes from literature and legends, as well as studies of plants and animals.

A mosque in northwestern India

Peasants working in a paddy (rice) field

The hajj
Every year devout Muslims made their way to Surat to board ships to Jiddah, in the Red Sea. From there, they walked the hajj—the pilgrimage journey to Mecca in the Middle East.

The British
The British East India Company was founded in 1600 to trade with eastern Asia. Later it turned its attention to India.

Growing food
Rice, grains, vegetables, and fruits, as well as cotton and other crops, were grown in the fertile Ganges river valley.

Growing rice
Rice was the main crop and foodstuff for many Indians. It was widely grown in the wet Ganges river delta.

Collaboration
Hindu merchants often cooperated with their fellow Hindu Marathas against their Muslim Mogul rulers. They gave them weapons to use to attack the Moguls.

Clive of India
Several victories by Robert Clive gave the British East India Company control of Bengal, Bihar, and a lot of the east coast by 1768. This marked the end of French power in India.

The Black Hole of Calcutta
In June 1756, 145 British prisoners were held in a small dungeon overnight by the Nawab (ruler) of Bengal. Only 23 of them survived.

Taj Mahal in Agra

KABUL

Kandahar

Amritsar

Panipat

DELHI

Agra

Benares

Plassey

Calcutta

Surat

Hindu Kush

Himalayas

Punjab

Oudh

Bihar

Bengal

Gujarat

Ganges

Yamuna

Indus

Mogul building

The Moguls were great builders, constructing many amazing palaces and mausoleums (tombs) surrounded by beautiful, water-filled gardens. The most famous of these buildings is the Taj Mahal (above), a mausoleum for Shah Jahan and his wife that was built in the 1630s in Agra. The Moguls also constructed entire new cities, including a new capital in Fatehpur Sikri, outside of Agra. This city was built by an order from the emperor Akbar I between 1571 and 1584, but people only lived there for 14 years because of its bad water supply. A new capital was later built in Delhi.

Cotton
The production of cotton cloth was a major industry in most of Mogul India. Women did most of the weaving.

The French
The French East India Company had its main base in Pondicherry, with other bases along the coast and inland in Bengal.

The Dutch
The Dutch East India Company set up bases around the coast of southern India, forcing the Portuguese out of Ceylon by 1660 and taking over the entire island by 1766.

Going native
European merchants adopted Indian customs and methods of transportation to give them authority over the local people.

Portuguese trading post in Goa

Mysore
The Muslim-run state of Mysore in the south of India was a major power in the region, resisting both Mogul and Maratha rule.

Goa
In 1510 the Portuguese set up Europe's first colony in Asia—in Goa.

Arab traders
Merchants from Arabia and east Africa traded gold, gems, ivory, and coffee across the Indian Ocean to India, in return for cotton, silk, spices, and dyes.

Vasco da Gama
The Portuguese navigator Vasco da Gama became the first European to reach India by sailing around the southern tip of Africa, landing in Cochin in May 1498.

The wealth of the empire

The Moguls ran an efficient banking system that was based on gold and silver coins, providing credit for merchants throughout Asia and east Africa. Trade with Arabs and Europeans across the Indian Ocean brought a lot of wealth to the empire. Mogul agriculture was strong, with greater grain harvests than in Europe, while their iron industry produced good quality steel. Mogul India also had the world's largest textile industry, exporting cotton goods worldwide.

MOGUL EMPIRE
Deccan
Golconda

Arabian Sea
Daman
• Bombay
• Goa
Calicut
Cochin
MYSORE
Trichinopoly
Pondicherry
Arcot
Madras
Ceylon

500km
250 miles
0
0

1501–1530 Reign of Babur, the first Mogul emperor
1504 Moguls conquer the region around Kabul
1510 Portuguese set up a trading post in Goa, with others in Diu and Daman
1519 Moguls' first raid on India
1526 Full-scale Mogul invasion of India

1539–1556 Suri Afghans of Bihar rebel and reclaim a lot of territory from the Moguls

1550

1556–1605 Reign of Akbar I

1572 Moguls conquer Gujarat, giving them access to the sea
1576 Moguls conquer Bengal, India's wealthiest territory

1600
1600 British East India Co. is founded
1602 Dutch East India Co. is founded
1605 Moguls advance south into the Deccan
1612 British East India Co. defeats a Portuguese fleet in Surat

1628–1658 Reign of Shah Jahan, who ordered the building of the Taj Mahal
1639–1648 New capital city constructed by the order of Shah Jahan in Shahjahanabad (Delhi)
1647–1680 Led by Sivaji, Hindu Marathas raid Mogul India

1650

1655–1660 Dutch seize bases in Ceylon from the Portuguese
1658–1707 Reign of Aurangzeb: Mogul Empire at its largest size
1661 British East India Co. establishes a base in Bombay
1664 French East India Co. is set up

1687 Moguls capture the southern state of Golconda

1700

1708 Marathas begin to conquer the Deccan

1739 Persian troops ransack the Mogul capital of Delhi
1740 War between Marathas and Moguls in southern India brings in the French and the British

1750

1751–1752 British under the command of Robert Clive score decisive victories against the French in Arcot and Trichinopoly
1757 Clive defeats Mogul Nawab (ruler) of Bengal in Plassey
1761 Maratha power ends after a massive defeat outside of Delhi by an Afghan army that later withdraws from India
1761 British seize Pondicherry, ending French power in India
1775 British control all of Bengal and Bihar
by 1800, Mogul Empire now only survives in name

1800

The Tudors and the Stuarts

Years of warfare in England between rival royal houses ended in 1485 when Henry VII became the first Tudor king. The Tudors were strong rulers who brought peace and prosperity to the country. Under King Henry VIII, England broke away from Rome and the Catholic Church and became increasingly Protestant. In 1603 the last Tudor monarch, Queen Elizabeth I, died. Elizabeth was succeeded by the Scottish king, James VI, from the Stuart family, who united England and Scotland for the first time. But the Stuarts were weak kings. One of them, King Charles I, was executed after a civil war, and another, King James II (James VII of Scotland), was driven into exile because he was a Catholic. Overseas trade, however, was slowly making Britain one of the wealthiest nations in Europe.

The English Civil War: a war of three kingdoms

Charles I was the king of England, Scotland, and Ireland. Each country had its own parliament, Church, and laws. Charles believed that he had a "divine right to rule," which was given to him by God, but his religious policies attracted opposition. A rebellion broke out in Scotland in 1639 and then in Ireland in 1641, before the king and Parliament clashed in England in 1642. Civil war raged in all three kingdoms before Charles was executed by the English Parliament in 1649 for waging war on his people. From 1649 to 1660, Britain was a republic (a nation without a monarch) for the only time in its history.

The Spanish Armada
Defeated in August 1588 (see page 23), the Spanish Armada was forced to sail around the rocky north and west coasts of Ireland and Scotland, where many ships were wrecked in storms.

Irish rebellions
Ireland was the only part of the British Isles that remained Catholic. This led to many rebellions against Ireland's Protestant and English rulers.

Union of the crowns
In 1603 the Stuart king of Scotland, James VI, became King James I of England. This united the two crowns, but both nations remained independent.

Suspicious murder
Lord Darnley, the husband of Mary, Queen of Scots, was killed in an explosion in Edinburgh, Scotland, in 1567. Mary was accused of being involved, but nothing was proved.

Flodden Field
The English defeat of the Scots in Flodden Field in 1513 weakened Scotland greatly and put it at the mercy of the English for the rest of the century.

Atlantic Ocean

SCOTLAND

■ EDINBURGH

Tweed

• Flodden

North Sea

• Londonderry

Ulster

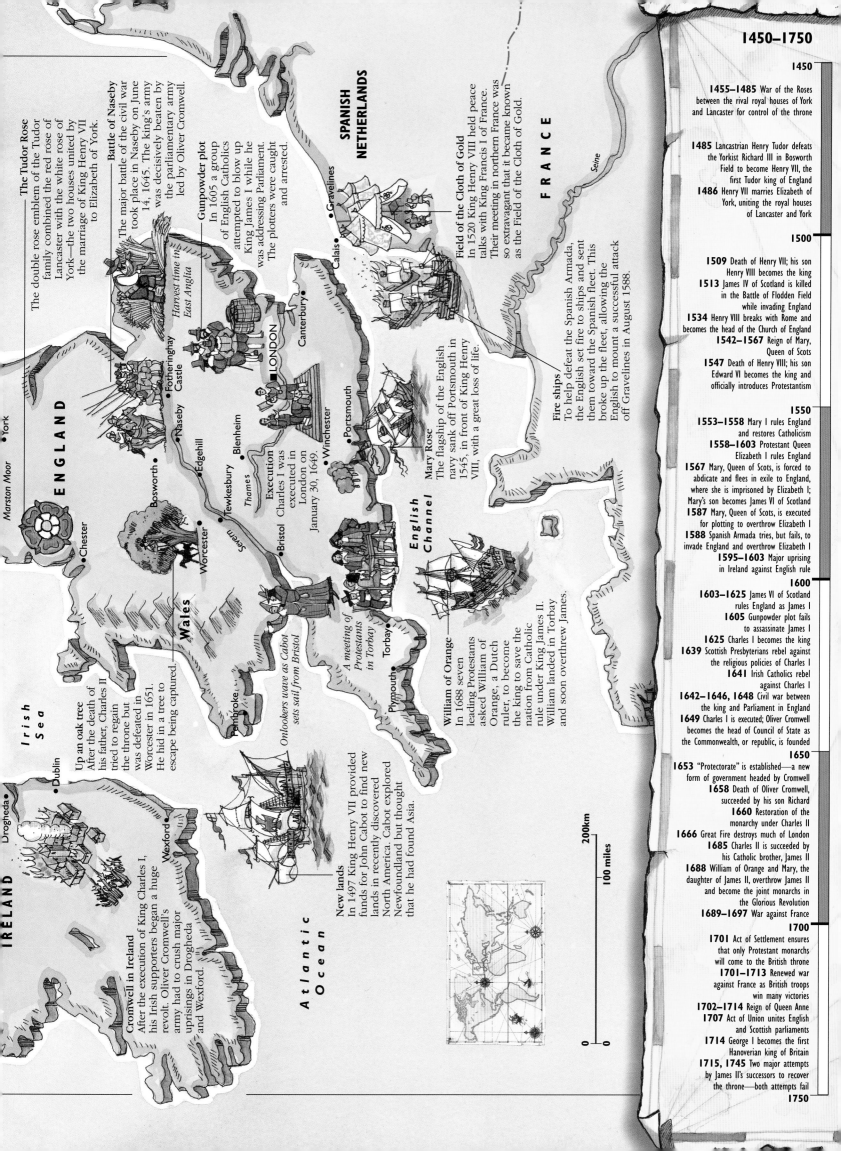

The Tudor Rose
The double rose emblem of the Tudor family combined the red rose of Lancaster with the white rose of York—the two houses united by the marriage of King Henry VII to Elizabeth of York.

Battle of Naseby
The major battle of the civil war took place in Naseby on June 14, 1645. The king's army was decisively beaten by the parliamentary army led by Oliver Cromwell.

Harvest time in East Anglia

Gunpowder plot
In 1605 a group of English Catholics attempted to blow up King James I while he was addressing Parliament. The plotters were caught and arrested.

SPANISH NETHERLANDS

Field of the Cloth of Gold
In 1520 King Henry VIII held peace talks with King Francis I of France. Their meeting in northern France was so extravagant that it became known as the Field of the Cloth of Gold.

F R A N C E

Seine

• Gravelines

Calais •

Canterbury •

Fire ships
To help defeat the Spanish Armada, the English set fire to ships and sent them toward the Spanish fleet. This broke up the fleet, allowing the English to mount a successful attack off Gravelines in August 1588.

• York

E N G L A N D

Marston Moor

• Chester

• Fotheringhay Castle

• Naseby

Bosworth •

• Edgehill

Blenheim •

LONDON

• Winchester

• Portsmouth

Mary Rose
The flagship of the English navy sank off Portsmouth in 1545, in front of King Henry VIII, with a great loss of life.

English Channel

Tewkesbury •

Thames

• Worcester

Severn

Bristol •

Execution
Charles I was executed in London on January 30, 1649.

Wales

Irish Sea

• Dublin

Drogheda •

I R E L A N D

Wexford •

Pembroke •

Cromwell in Ireland
After the execution of King Charles I, his Irish supporters began a huge revolt. Oliver Cromwell's army had to crush major uprisings in Drogheda and Wexford.

Up an oak tree
After the death of his father, Charles II tried to regain the throne but was defeated in Worcester in 1651. He hid in a tree to escape being captured.

Onlookers wave as Cabot sets sail from Bristol

A meeting of Protestants in Torbay

• Torbay

• Plymouth

William of Orange
In 1688 seven leading Protestants asked William of Orange, a Dutch ruler, to become the king to save the nation from Catholic rule under King James II. William landed in Torbay and soon overthrew James.

New lands
In 1497 King Henry VII provided funds for John Cabot to find new lands in recently discovered North America. Cabot explored Newfoundland but thought that he had found Asia.

Atlantic Ocean

200km

100 miles

0   0

1455–1485 War of the Roses between the rival royal houses of York and Lancaster for control of the throne

1485 Lancastrian Henry Tudor defeats the Yorkist Richard III in Bosworth Field to become Henry VII, the first Tudor king of England
1486 Henry VII marries Elizabeth of York, uniting the royal houses of Lancaster and York

1500

1509 Death of Henry VII; his son Henry VIII becomes the king
1513 James IV of Scotland is killed in the Battle of Flodden Field while invading England
1534 Henry VIII breaks with Rome and becomes the head of the Church of England
1542–1567 Reign of Mary, Queen of Scots
1547 Death of Henry VIII; his son Edward VI becomes the king and officially introduces Protestantism

1550

1553–1558 Mary I rules England and restores Catholicism
1558–1603 Protestant Queen Elizabeth I rules England
1567 Mary, Queen of Scots, is forced to abdicate and flees in exile to England, where she is imprisoned by Elizabeth I; Mary's son becomes James VI of Scotland
1587 Mary, Queen of Scots, is executed for plotting to overthrow Elizabeth I
1588 Spanish Armada tries, but fails, to invade England and overthrow Elizabeth I
1595–1603 Major uprising in Ireland against English rule

1600

1603–1625 James VI of Scotland rules England as James I
1605 Gunpowder plot fails to assassinate James I
1625 Charles I becomes the king
1639 Scottish Presbyterians rebel against the religious policies of Charles I
1641 Irish Catholics rebel against Charles I
1642–1646, 1648 Civil war between the king and Parliament in England
1649 Charles I is executed; Oliver Cromwell becomes the head of Council of State as the Commonwealth, or republic, is founded

1650

1653 "Protectorate" is established—a new form of government headed by Cromwell
1658 Death of Oliver Cromwell, succeeded by his son Richard
1660 Restoration of the monarchy under Charles II
1666 Great Fire destroys much of London
1685 Charles II is succeeded by his Catholic brother, James II
1688 William of Orange and Mary, the daughter of James II, overthrow James II and become the joint monarchs in the Glorious Revolution
1689–1697 War against France

1700

1701 Act of Settlement ensures that only Protestant monarchs will come to the British throne
1701–1713 Renewed war against France as British troops win many victories
1702–1714 Reign of Queen Anne
1707 Act of Union unites English and Scottish parliaments
1714 George I becomes the first Hanoverian king of Britain
1715, 1745 Two major attempts by James II's successors to recover the throne—both attempts fail

1750

Divided Europe

After the religious turmoil of the Reformation a brief period of peace descended on Europe in the 1550s. However, the differences between Protestants and Catholics continued to divide the continent, causing civil war in France and a revolt in the Netherlands against Spanish rule. A major conflict also broke out for control of the Baltic Sea. In 1618 Protestant-Catholic rivalries in Germany led to a war that soon spread across the rest of Europe. By the end of the war, Germany was devastated, Spain lost its leadership of Catholic Europe to France, Sweden dominated northern Europe and the Baltic, and the Dutch were independent and wealthy.

dotted lines show the borders between European countries in 1648

Dutch domination
Dutch merchants controlled trade in both the North and Baltic seas. By 1650, Dutch businessmen dominated Europe's entire economy.

Reclaiming the sea
The Dutch built dykes (flood barriers) and used windmills to reclaim land from the sea. They lived on this land and grew food there.

Peace of Westphalia
The Thirty Years' War ended in 1648, when a peace treaty was signed in the German state of Westphalia.

Civil war
England, Scotland, and Ireland were all involved in civil wars from 1639–1651, keeping them out of the European conflicts.

Frost fairs
The Thames river froze over during most winters as a mini ice age engulfed Europe. Many Londoners sold their wares on the ice.

Henry IV
The conversion of the French king Henry IV from Protestantism to Catholicism, in 1593, led to the end of the wars of religion in France.

La Rochelle
French Protestant Huguenots rose up in revolt again in 1620, but they were crushed when their stronghold in La Rochelle was successfully besieged.

Cardinal Richelieu
From 1624–1642, Cardinal Richelieu ran the government for Louis XIII. He crushed the Huguenots and built up French military strength against Spain.

Portugal in revolt
Spain took control of Portugal by force in 1580. Sixty years later the Portuguese rose up in revolt and, with help from the French, won back their independence.

Escorial Palace
The huge Escorial Palace outside of Madrid was built for Philip II in 1563–1584. He ruled his large European and American empire from there.

Catalonia
In 1640 the French supported a revolt in Catalonia against Spanish rule. The region came under the protection of Louis XIII until the revolt was crushed in the 1650s.

NORWAY

SCOTLAND

North Sea

IRELAND

ENGLAND

LONDON

UNITED PROVINCES

AMSTERDAM

Emden

Dutch delft pottery

Westphalia

Antwerp

SPANISH NETHERLANDS

Rocroi

Seine

PARIS

Nantes

Loire

FRANCE

La Rochelle

SWITZERLAND

Atlantic Ocean

Douro

Ebro

MADRID

Tagus

LISBON

PORTUGAL

SPAIN

Catalonia

Sardinia

Guadalquivir

Mediterranean Sea

0   500km
0   250 miles

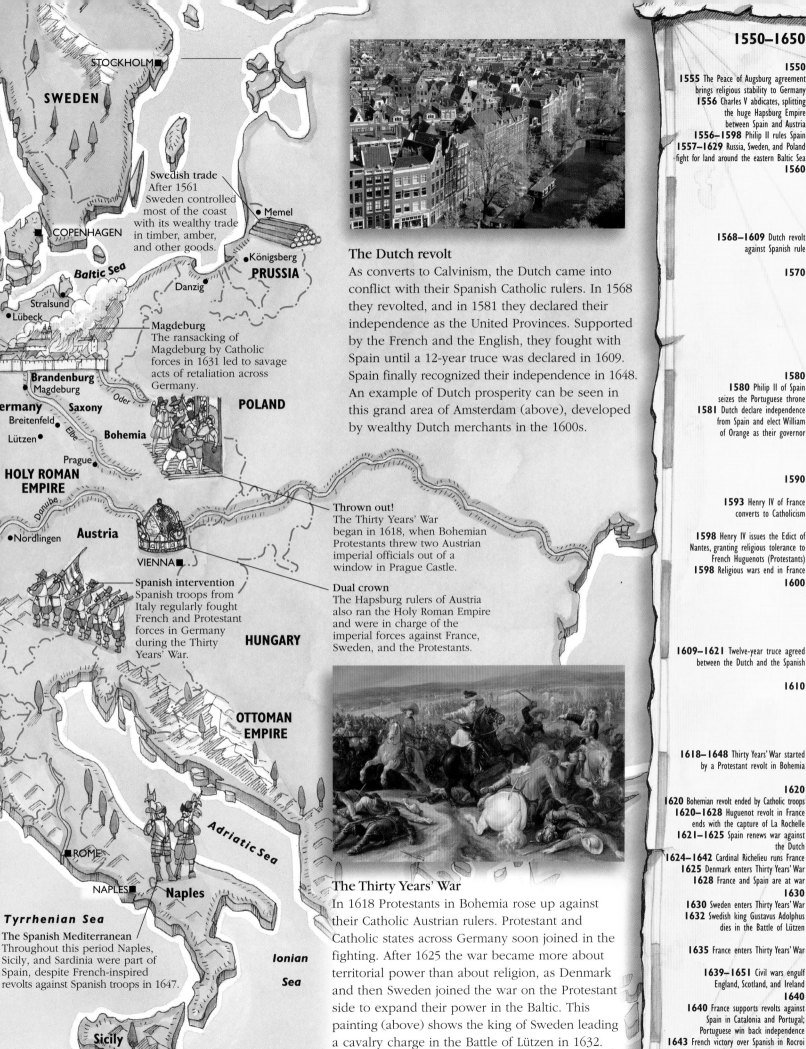

STOCKHOLM

SWEDEN

COPENHAGEN

Baltic Sea

Stralsund
Lübeck

• Memel

• Königsberg
PRUSSIA
Danzig

Swedish trade
After 1561 Sweden controlled most of the coast with its wealthy trade in timber, amber, and other goods.

Magdeburg
The ransacking of Magdeburg by Catholic forces in 1631 led to savage acts of retaliation across Germany.

Brandenburg
Magdeburg
Oder
Germany   Saxony
Breitenfeld •
Lützen •   Elbe   **Bohemia**
Prague •

POLAND

HOLY ROMAN EMPIRE
Danube

Nordlingen •   **Austria**

VIENNA

Spanish intervention
Spanish troops from Italy regularly fought French and Protestant forces in Germany during the Thirty Years' War.

HUNGARY

Thrown out!
The Thirty Years' War began in 1618, when Bohemian Protestants threw two Austrian imperial officials out of a window in Prague Castle.

Dual crown
The Hapsburg rulers of Austria also ran the Holy Roman Empire and were in charge of the imperial forces against France, Sweden, and the Protestants.

OTTOMAN EMPIRE

Adriatic Sea

ROME

NAPLES   **Naples**

Tyrrhenian Sea

The Spanish Mediterranean
Throughout this period Naples, Sicily, and Sardinia were part of Spain, despite French-inspired revolts against Spanish troops in 1647.

Ionian Sea

Sicily

The Dutch revolt

As converts to Calvinism, the Dutch came into conflict with their Spanish Catholic rulers. In 1568 they revolted, and in 1581 they declared their independence as the United Provinces. Supported by the French and the English, they fought with Spain until a 12-year truce was declared in 1609. Spain finally recognized their independence in 1648. An example of Dutch prosperity can be seen in this grand area of Amsterdam (above), developed by wealthy Dutch merchants in the 1600s.

The Thirty Years' War

In 1618 Protestants in Bohemia rose up against their Catholic Austrian rulers. Protestant and Catholic states across Germany soon joined in the fighting. After 1625 the war became more about territorial power than about religion, as Denmark and then Sweden joined the war on the Protestant side to expand their power in the Baltic. This painting (above) shows the king of Sweden leading a cavalry charge in the Battle of Lützen in 1632.

The expansion of Russia

Over the course of 300 years, the small, poor, landlocked state of Muscovy expanded to become Russia—one of the major nations in Europe. In order to do this, it had to overcome huge problems—a small population, huge distances between towns, a terrible climate, and large areas of empty land in which hostile armies could easily hide. The main driving force behind Russia's success was Peter the Great, who modeled Russia on the western countries of Europe and almost single-handedly modernized the nation. Victories over Sweden, by 1721, gave Russia access to the Baltic Sea, paving the way for future Russian success and territorial gains during the 1700s.

The Ural Mountains
The Ural Mountains form the border between Europe and Asia. During the late 1500s, the Russians crossed these mountains and built many new towns in Siberia.

Polar bear roaming the Arctic tundra

Building St. Petersburg
In 1703 work began on a new capital city, which gave access to the Baltic Sea.

Metal working
Many new state-owned iron and copper works were built in the Ural Mountains to exploit the great mineral wealth of the mountains.

Moscow
After the fall of Constantinople to the Muslim Ottomans in 1453, Moscow became the center of Orthodox Christianity in Europe.

Close shave
To make his country more like those in the West, Peter the Great ordered all of his lords and nobles to shave off their beards and dress in Western clothing.

Russian navy
Peter the Great studied shipbuilding in England, returning home in 1698 to create a great navy.

International trade
Russian merchants traded silk, tea, and gems from China and textiles from Persia and central Asia. Sugar, tobacco, and wine were imported from Europe.

Fur trading
During the 1600s, in order to develop the local fur trade, a series of fortified trading stations were built along the main trade route to China.

Serfs (peasants) working on a farm

Controlling the Caspian
In 1723 Russian troops occupied the western and southern coasts of the Caspian Sea, but the Persians forced them to give up these areas in 1732.

SWEDEN
ST. PETERSBURG
Karelia
Ingria
Narva
Estonia
Novgorod
Pskov
Livonia
Baltic Sea
Moscow
Smolensk
Kazan
POLAND
Kiev
Don
Dnieper
Poltava
Astrakhan
Azov
KHANATE OF CRIMEA
Sevastopol
Caucasus Mountains
Black Sea
Caspian Sea
Constantinople
OTTOMAN EMPIRE
SAFAVID EMPIRE
Ural Mountains
RUSSIA
Siberia
Tobolsk
Tomsk
Yeniseysk
Krasnoyarsk
Irkutsk
Kyakht

The city of Peter the Great

Peter the Great wanted to give Russia "a window on the West" so that it could trade ideas, goods, and technology with western Europe. In 1703 he ordered the construction of a new city—St. Petersburg—on marshland next to the Neva river at the eastern end of the Baltic Sea. Many thousands of workers died building the city, which includes the Winter Palace (left) and other grand buildings. St. Petersburg became the national capital of Russia in 1712, as well as one of the leading cultural and diplomatic cities in Europe.

Arctic Ocean

Fur trapping
Siberian tribesmen hunted bears and other animals for their meat and fur. They traded these goods with Russian merchants in return for guns and other items.

Felling trees for timber

Bering Strait

Alaska

Crossing to North America
Russian traders crossed the Bering Strait into Alaska, and in 1784 they established the first Russian settlement there. Alaska was sold to the U.S. in 1867.

Amur

Amur

CHINA

Pacific Ocean

Fortifying the border
In 1650 Russian troops occupied the Amur region, north of China and built forts along the Amur river border. The region was returned to China in 1689.

dotted line shows the extent of Russian territory in 1783

| 0 | | 500km |
| 0 | | 250 miles |

1450–1800

1450

1478 Led by Ivan III, "the Great," Muscovy conquers its main rival, Novgorod
1480 Muscovy becomes independent of Mongol Tatar rule

1500

1501 Ivan III expands his territory west, toward Poland

1533–1584 Reign of Ivan IV, "the Terrible"

1547 Ivan IV is crowned the first czar (emperor) of Russia

1550

1552 Russia begins to conquer Tatar khanates north of the Caspian Sea

1581 Russia begins to expand over the Ural Mountains and into Siberia
1582 Poland and Sweden prevent Russia from gaining access to the Baltic Sea

1600

1613–1645 Reign of Mikhail I, the first czar of the Romanov family

1637 Russian explorers reach the Pacific coast of Siberia for the first time

1650

1650–1689 Russian occupation of the Amur region, north of China

1682–1725 Reign of Peter I, "the Great"

1696 Russia captures Azov from the Ottomans, giving it access to the Black Sea
1697–1698 Peter I travels around western Europe, studying new ideas on how to modernize his country

1700

1700–1721 Great Northern War with Sweden brings Russia land around the Baltic Sea
1703 Construction of St. Petersburg begins

1712 National capital moved from Moscow to St. Petersburg

1750

1762–1792 Reign of Catherine II, "the Great"
1768–1774 War against the Ottomans brings gains around the Black Sea
1772 First Partition of Poland: Russia, Austria, and Prussia seize Polish territory; Russian frontier extends west
1783 Russia captures the Crimea
1784 Russians establish their first settlement in Alaska

1800

China and Japan

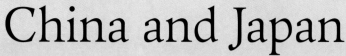

In 1368 the Chinese Ming dynasty replaced the foreign-born Mongols as the rulers in the region. In 1644 the Ming dynasty was replaced by another foreign dynasty, the Manchus, who came from the northern region of Manchuria. The Manchus quickly adopted Chinese fashions—shaving their heads and wearing pigtails—but most importantly, they turned China into a dynamic, efficient state of incredible power and wealth. Neighboring states, such as Korea, came under the control of the Chinese. Japan remained independent, ruled in name by an emperor but ruled in reality by powerful shoguns (military warlords). European contact with China and Japan was very limited.

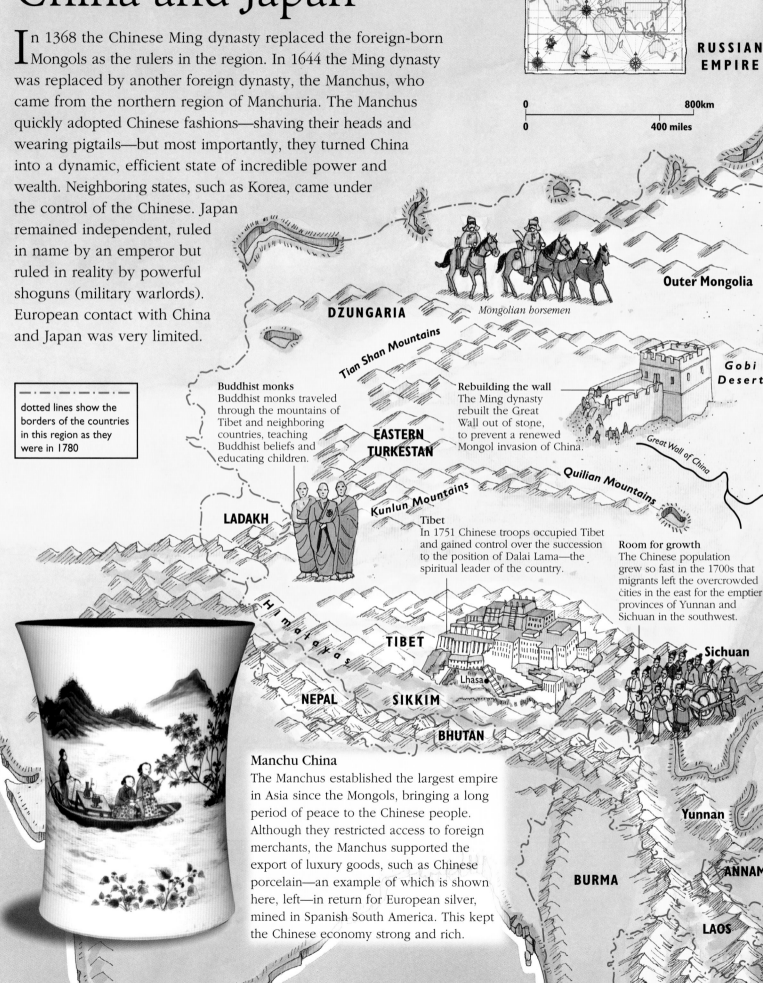

RUSSIAN EMPIRE

0   800km
0   400 miles

dotted lines show the borders of the countries in this region as they were in 1780

Mongolian horsemen

Outer Mongolia

DZUNGARIA

Tian Shan Mountains

Gobi Desert

Buddhist monks
Buddhist monks traveled through the mountains of Tibet and neighboring countries, teaching Buddhist beliefs and educating children.

EASTERN TURKESTAN

Rebuilding the wall
The Ming dynasty rebuilt the Great Wall out of stone, to prevent a renewed Mongol invasion of China.

Great Wall of China

Quilian Mountains

Kunlun Mountains

LADAKH

Tibet
In 1751 Chinese troops occupied Tibet and gained control over the succession to the position of Dalai Lama—the spiritual leader of the country.

Room for growth
The Chinese population grew so fast in the 1700s that migrants left the overcrowded cities in the east for the emptier provinces of Yunnan and Sichuan in the southwest.

Himalayas

TIBET

Lhasa

Sichuan

NEPAL   **SIKKIM**

BHUTAN

Manchu China
The Manchus established the largest empire in Asia since the Mongols, bringing a long period of peace to the Chinese people. Although they restricted access to foreign merchants, the Manchus supported the export of luxury goods, such as Chinese porcelain—an example of which is shown here, left—in return for European silver, mined in Spanish South America. This kept the Chinese economy strong and rich.

Yunnan

BURMA

ANNAM

LAOS

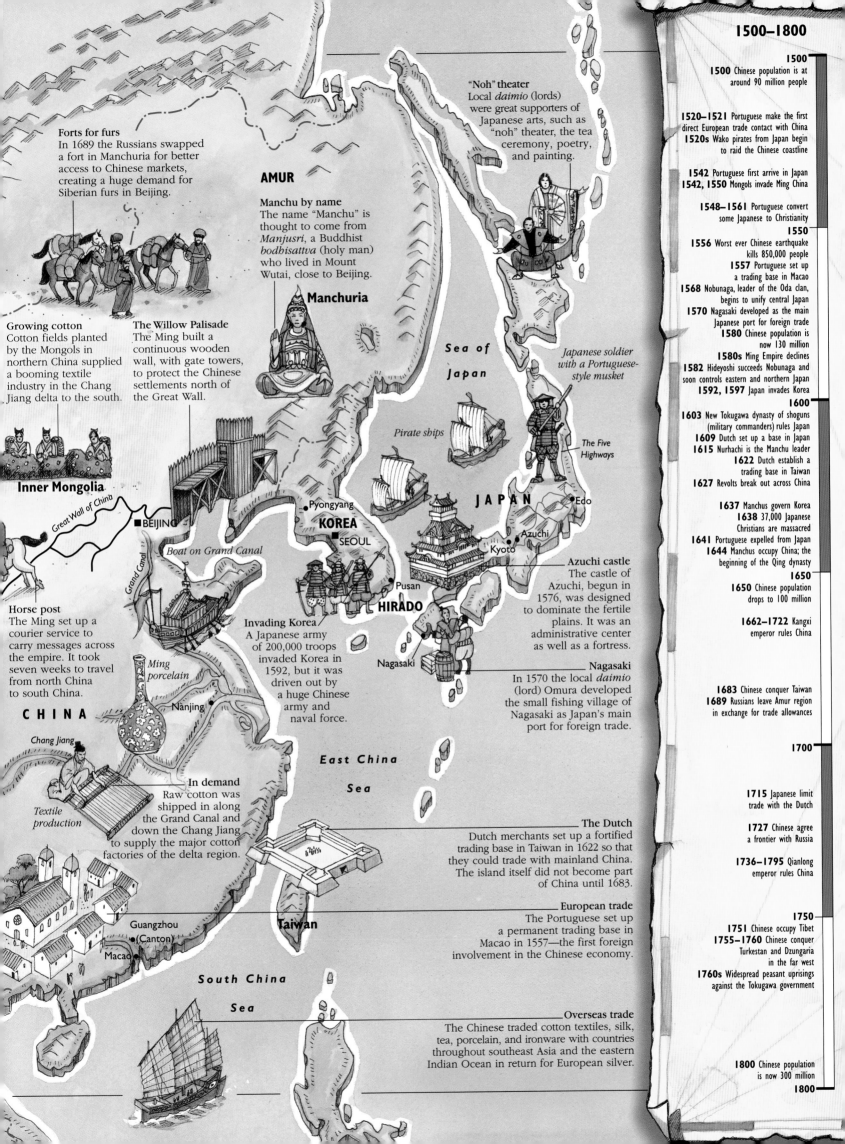

Forts for furs
In 1689 the Russians swapped a fort in Manchuria for better access to Chinese markets, creating a huge demand for Siberian furs in Beijing.

AMUR

Manchu by name
The name "Manchu" is thought to come from *Manjusri*, a Buddhist *bodhisattva* (holy man) who lived in Mount Wutai, close to Beijing.

"Noh" theater
Local *daimio* (lords) were great supporters of Japanese arts, such as "noh" theater, the tea ceremony, poetry, and painting.

Manchuria

Growing cotton
Cotton fields planted by the Mongols in northern China supplied a booming textile industry in the Chang Jiang delta to the south.

The Willow Palisade
The Ming built a continuous wooden wall, with gate towers, to protect the Chinese settlements north of the Great Wall.

Sea of Japan

Japanese soldier with a Portuguese-style musket

Inner Mongolia

Pirate ships

Great Wall of China

■BEIJING

Boat on Grand Canal

● Pyongyang

KOREA

■ SEOUL

JAPAN

●Edo

● Azuchi

Kyoto

The Five Highways

Horse post
The Ming set up a courier service to carry messages across the empire. It took seven weeks to travel from north China to south China.

Grand Canal

● Pusan

HIRADO

Azuchi castle
The castle of Azuchi, begun in 1576, was designed to dominate the fertile plains. It was an administrative center as well as a fortress.

Ming porcelain

Invading Korea
A Japanese army of 200,000 troops invaded Korea in 1592, but it was driven out by a huge Chinese army and naval force.

Nagasaki

Nagasaki
In 1570 the local *daimio* (lord) Omura developed the small fishing village of Nagasaki as Japan's main port for foreign trade.

CHINA

● Nanjing

Chang Jiang

Textile production

In demand
Raw cotton was shipped in along the Grand Canal and down the Chang Jiang to supply the major cotton factories of the delta region.

East China Sea

The Dutch
Dutch merchants set up a fortified trading base in Taiwan in 1622 so that they could trade with mainland China. The island itself did not become part of China until 1683.

European trade
The Portuguese set up a permanent trading base in Macao in 1557—the first foreign involvement in the Chinese economy.

Guangzhou (Canton)

Taiwan

Macao ●

South China Sea

Overseas trade
The Chinese traded cotton textiles, silk, tea, porcelain, and ironware with countries throughout southeast Asia and the eastern Indian Ocean in return for European silver.

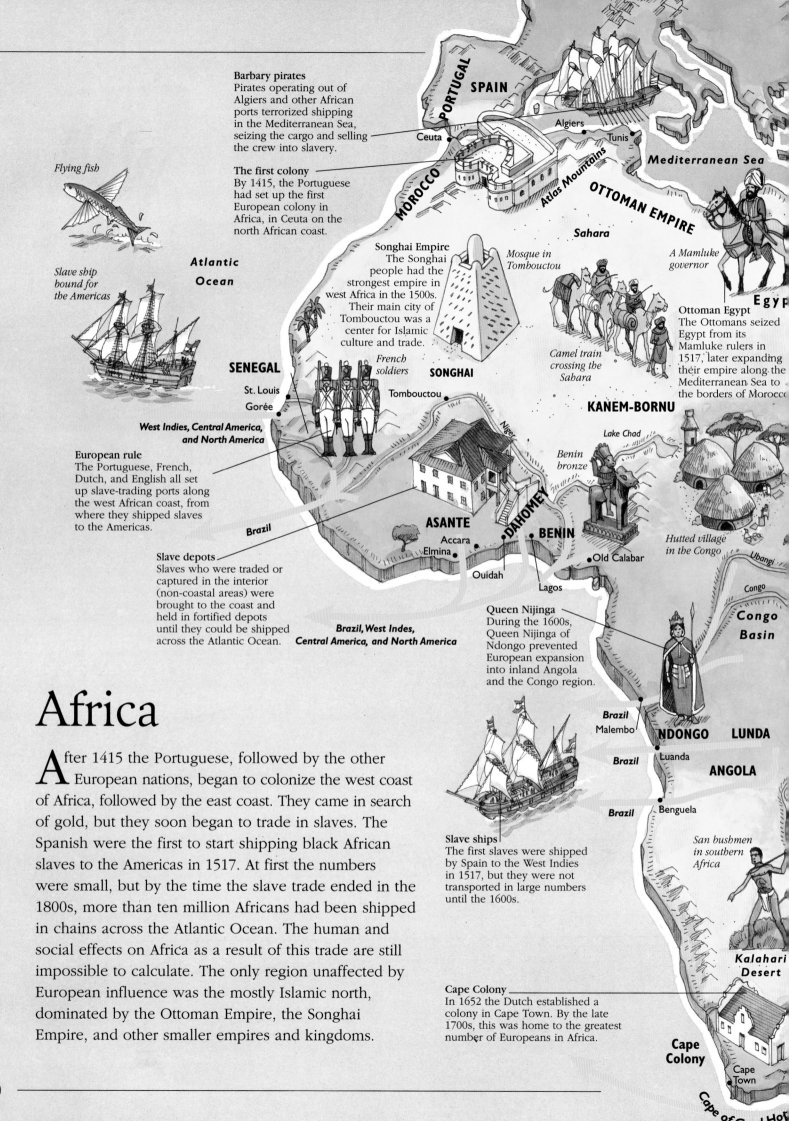

Barbary pirates
Pirates operating out of Algiers and other African ports terrorized shipping in the Mediterranean Sea, seizing the cargo and selling the crew into slavery.

The first colony
By 1415, the Portuguese had set up the first European colony in Africa, in Ceuta on the north African coast.

Flying fish

Slave ship bound for the Americas

Atlantic Ocean

PORTUGAL SPAIN

Ceuta Algiers Tunis

Mediterranean Sea

MOROCCO Atlas Mountains OTTOMAN EMPIRE

Sahara

A Mamluke governor

Songhai Empire
The Songhai people had the strongest empire in west Africa in the 1500s. Their main city of Tombouctou was a center for Islamic culture and trade.

Mosque in Tombouctou

Ottoman Egypt
The Ottomans seized Egypt from its Mamluke rulers in 1517, later expanding their empire along the Mediterranean Sea to the borders of Morocco.

Egypt

SENEGAL

St. Louis
Gorée

French soldiers SONGHAI

Tombouctou

Camel train crossing the Sahara

KANEM-BORNU

West Indies, Central America, and North America

European rule
The Portuguese, French, Dutch, and English all set up slave-trading ports along the west African coast, from where they shipped slaves to the Americas.

Lake Chad

Benin bronze

Brazil

ASANTE DAHOMEY BENIN

Accara
Elmina

Ouidah

Lagos

Old Calabar

Hutted village in the Congo

Ubangi

Congo

Congo Basin

Slave depots
Slaves who were traded or captured in the interior (non-coastal areas) were brought to the coast and held in fortified depots until they could be shipped across the Atlantic Ocean.

Brazil, West Indes, Central America, and North America

Queen Nijinga
During the 1600s, Queen Nijinga of Ndongo prevented European expansion into inland Angola and the Congo region.

Brazil
Malembo

NDONGO LUNDA

Brazil Luanda

ANGOLA

Brazil Benguela

San bushmen in southern Africa

Slave ships
The first slaves were shipped by Spain to the West Indies in 1517, but they were not transported in large numbers until the 1600s.

Africa

After 1415 the Portuguese, followed by the other European nations, began to colonize the west coast of Africa, followed by the east coast. They came in search of gold, but they soon began to trade in slaves. The Spanish were the first to start shipping black African slaves to the Americas in 1517. At first the numbers were small, but by the time the slave trade ended in the 1800s, more than ten million Africans had been shipped in chains across the Atlantic Ocean. The human and social effects on Africa as a result of this trade are still impossible to calculate. The only region unaffected by European influence was the mostly Islamic north, dominated by the Ottoman Empire, the Songhai Empire, and other smaller empires and kingdoms.

Cape Colony
In 1652 the Dutch established a colony in Cape Town. By the late 1700s, this was home to the greatest number of Europeans in Africa.

Kalahari Desert

Cape Colony

Cape Town

Cape of Good Hope

The Portuguese east coast

In 1498 the Portuguese navigator Vasco da Gama sailed around the Cape of Good Hope on his way to India. This opened up a new trade route between Europe and India across the Indian Ocean. The Portuguese soon set up a series of trading bases along the east coast such as in Kilwa (left). These bases stretched from Delagoa Bay in the south to the island of Socotra, at the mouth of the Red Sea, in the north.

Jesuit conversions
Jesuit missionaries arrived in Ethiopia in 1557 to convert the Ethiopians from the Coptic Church to the Roman Catholic Church.

Arabian Peninsula

Arabian Sea

India

ETHIOPIA

ADAL

Arab traders
Arab dhows (sailing boats) traded goods with India, the Arabian Peninsula, and the Persian Gulf, often in competition and conflict with their Portuguese rivals.

Socotra

Waina Dega

Lake Turkana

Rift Valley

Mogadishu

Lake Victoria

SULTANATE OF ZANZIBAR

Lake Tanganyika

Rift Valley

Malindi
Mombasa
Zanzibar
Kilwa

Lake Nyasa

Great Mosque in Kilwa

Christians united
The Portuguese sent an army to help their fellow Christian Ethiopians defeat an invading Adali army in Waina Dega in 1543.

Portuguese trade
After 1505 the Portuguese set up a series of trading bases along the east African coast. From there, they traded gold, ivory, and spices across the Indian Ocean.

Indian Ocean

Gold
The Shona and Makua people mined and panned for gold close to Lake Nyasa. They traded it for guns, textiles, and other goods with Arab and Portuguese merchants along the coast.

Mozambique

Madagascar

MWENEMUTAPA

Zambezi

Limpopo

Delagoa Bay

Brazil

these arrows show the direction and destinations of the slave ships that sailed across the Atlantic Ocean from African ports

Cairo

Nile

| 0 | | 2,000km |
| 0 | | 1,000 miles |

The slave trade:
The terrible trade in humans

Slavery has existed throughout human history, but in the 1500s a new and terrible chapter in the story began. In 1502 a Portuguese ship transported west African slaves to the Americas. Regular shipments then started up in 1517. At first this trade was slow, but the increasing demand for labor on the new sugar plantations and in the mines outgrew the supply of Native Americans. So Africans were brought across the Atlantic Ocean to fill the gap. The trade flourished during the 1600s and 1700s, with approximately ten million Africans enslaved before the trade ended in the 1800s. The human cost of slavery was huge, and while it brought great wealth to European traders and North American landowners, it devastated Africa.

Trading in lives
Slaves who were captured during warfare between rival African kingdoms or enslaved by their own leaders were taken to the coast and sold to European slavers (slave traders). The picture above shows a man buying slaves in Gorée, a French island off Senegal on the west African coast. There the slaves were branded (marked with hot irons) and imprisoned in slave depots until a ship arrived to take them to the Americas.

On the plantation
Life on the plantations, such as this sugar plantation in Antigua in the West Indies, was harsh. Slaves were the property of the plantation owner and had no rights of their own. They worked long hours, often from sunrise until sunset, and were often whipped to make them work harder. They did not earn any money but were given enough food to keep them alive.

Male and female slaves hoed the land in a line, making it ready for planting sugar cane

Even young slave children were forced to work on the land

The overseer made sure that the slaves worked hard for their master

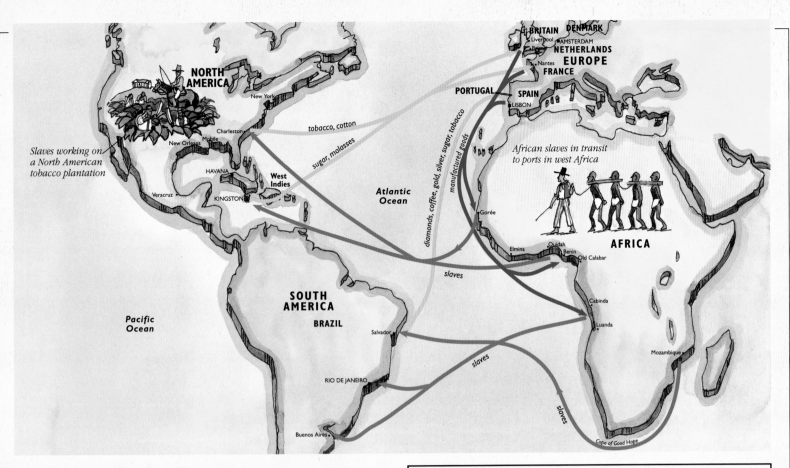

Slaves working on a North American tobacco plantation

African slaves in transit to ports in west Africa

The slave trade triangle

As shown in this map (above), the path of slave ships formed a triangular pattern across the Atlantic Ocean. Ships carrying manufactured goods, such as guns and cotton cloth, sailed from western European ports to the west African coast. There, the cargo was traded for slaves, who were then shipped across to Brazil, the West Indies, Central America, and North America. The slaves were sold to the plantation owners, and the ships returned home with a rich cargo of sugar, rum, tobacco, cotton, coffee, and sometimes silver and precious stones.

Remembering the past

Slavery ended during the 1800s, but its impact is still with us today. The economy and social structure of a lot of Africa has never recovered from the removal of so many young men and women as slaves, while the free descendants of slaves, especially in the U.S., still face unfair treatment and discrimination. This statue (right) is a memorial to those who were slaves in Barbados, a British island in the West Indies.

KEY TO MAP: THE "TRIANGULAR TRADE"

Ships carry manufactured goods from Europe to Africa →

The Middle Passage: Slaves are taken across the Atlantic Ocean →

Ships return home with raw materials from the Americas →

The Middle Passage

The voyage across the Atlantic Ocean from Africa to the Americas—known as the Middle Passage—took up to 16 weeks. Conditions onboard were appalling. Hundreds of slaves were tightly packed into the hold, as this painting shows (above). They were all chained together to stop them from jumping overboard. As many as four out of every ten slaves died making the journey across.

Colonizing North America

When Europeans first arrived in North America, the land puzzled them. The early explorers thought that it was Asia and did not realize that it was a continent in its own right, while Spanish conquistadors (conquerors) expected to discover gold-filled cities just like they had found earlier in Mexico and Peru. None of them realized just how big or potentially rich and fertile this continent was. But, slowly, Europeans began to colonize this new world—the French and English trapping and trading furs in the north, while farmers from all nations settled in colonies along the east coast. Once the barrier of the Appalachian Mountains was crossed in 1671, the way was clear for pioneer settlers to exploit this fertile land to the full.

Henry Hudson
In 1611 Hudson went in search of the Northwest Passage to the Pacific Ocean but his crew staged a mutiny. Hudson, his young son, and seven loyal sailors were left to die in a small boat.

Canada

Lake Winnipeg

The Great Lakes

Lake Superior

Hudson's Bay Company
After 1670 the English Hudson's Bay Company set up bases around Hudson Bay to trade furs with the native Cree people. The French captured all of the bases in 1686.

Rocky Mountains

Buffalo grazing

Hunting buffalo
The Plains Indians hunted herds of buffalo for their meat, skins, and bones.

New Mexico
The Spaniards set up a permanent base in Santa Fe in 1609, but their settlement in the region was limited by the harsh climate.

Great Plains

Mississippi

New Mexico

Tents of the Plains Indians

In search of gold
From 1539–1543, the Spaniard Hernando de Soto led an expedition up the Mississippi river in search of gold, inflicting great cruelty on the Native Americans that he met along his way.

• Santa Fe

Spanish pueblo village in the southwest

The first settlers

The first European settlers, such as those shown in this painting (above), inhabited the eastern coastline of North America— the Spaniards in the south, the English, Dutch, and Swedes in the center, and the French in the north and along the Saint Lawrence river. Many of the settlers had fled religious or political persecution in Europe and hoped to create a new life in a new world. They survived by growing their own crops and raising livestock, as well as by trading with the local Native Americans. They also received some supplies by ship from Europe.

Down river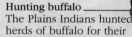
In 1682 Robert de la Salle became the first person to canoe down the Mississippi river. He was disappointed to find that it ended up in the Gulf of Mexico, and not in the Pacific Ocean.

Louisiana

Spanish explorers
In the 1500s Spain mounted huge military expeditions from Mexico and the Caribbean into North America in search of gold, as well as to convert the natives to Christianity. They did not succeed.

Mexico

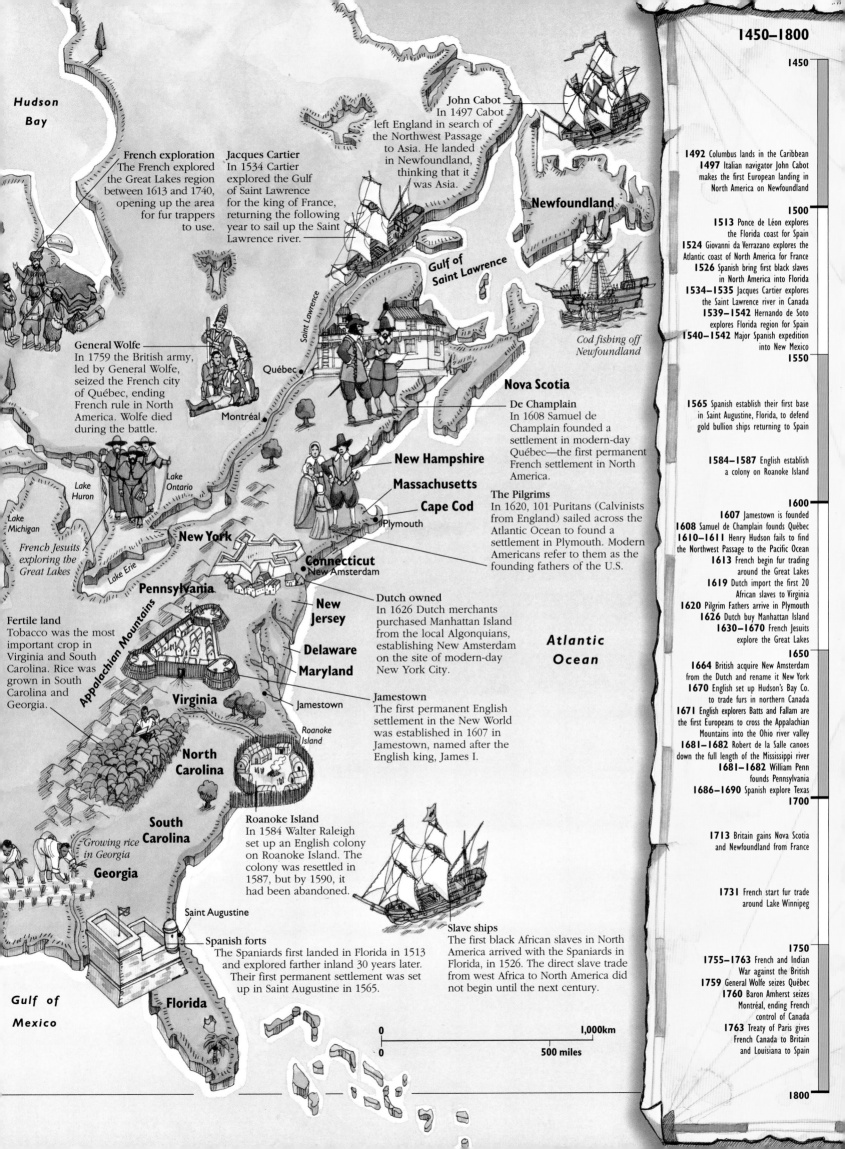

Hudson Bay

French exploration
The French explored the Great Lakes region between 1613 and 1740, opening up the area for fur trappers to use.

Jacques Cartier
In 1534 Cartier explored the Gulf of Saint Lawrence for the king of France, returning the following year to sail up the Saint Lawrence river.

John Cabot
In 1497 Cabot left England in search of the Northwest Passage to Asia. He landed in Newfoundland, thinking that it was Asia.

Newfoundland

Gulf of Saint Lawrence

Cod fishing off Newfoundland

General Wolfe
In 1759 the British army, led by General Wolfe, seized the French city of Québec, ending French rule in North America. Wolfe died during the battle.

Québec

Montréal

Nova Scotia

De Champlain
In 1608 Samuel de Champlain founded a settlement in modern-day Québec—the first permanent French settlement in North America.

French Jesuits exploring the Great Lakes

Lake Huron

Lake Ontario

Lake Michigan

Lake Erie

New Hampshire

Massachusetts

Cape Cod

Plymouth

The Pilgrims
In 1620, 101 Puritans (Calvinists from England) sailed across the Atlantic Ocean to found a settlement in Plymouth. Modern Americans refer to them as the founding fathers of the U.S.

New York

Connecticut
New Amsterdam

Pennsylvania

Appalachian Mountains

New Jersey

Delaware

Maryland

Dutch owned
In 1626 Dutch merchants purchased Manhattan Island from the local Algonquians, establishing New Amsterdam on the site of modern-day New York City.

Atlantic Ocean

Fertile land
Tobacco was the most important crop in Virginia and South Carolina. Rice was grown in South Carolina and Georgia.

Virginia

Jamestown

Roanoke Island

Jamestown
The first permanent English settlement in the New World was established in 1607 in Jamestown, named after the English king, James I.

North Carolina

South Carolina

Growing rice in Georgia

Georgia

Roanoke Island
In 1584 Walter Raleigh set up an English colony on Roanoke Island. The colony was resettled in 1587, but by 1590, it had been abandoned.

Saint Augustine

Spanish forts
The Spaniards first landed in Florida in 1513 and explored farther inland 30 years later. Their first permanent settlement was set up in Saint Augustine in 1565.

Slave ships
The first black African slaves in North America arrived with the Spaniards in Florida, in 1526. The direct slave trade from west Africa to North America did not begin until the next century.

Gulf of Mexico

Florida

0   1,000km

0   500 miles

1450

1492 Columbus lands in the Caribbean
1497 Italian navigator John Cabot makes the first European landing in North America on Newfoundland

1500

1513 Ponce de Léon explores the Florida coast for Spain
1524 Giovanni da Verrazano explores the Atlantic coast of North America for France
1526 Spanish bring first black slaves in North America into Florida
1534–1535 Jacques Cartier explores the Saint Lawrence river in Canada
1539–1542 Hernando de Soto explores Florida region for Spain
1540–1542 Major Spanish expedition into New Mexico

1550

1565 Spanish establish their first base in Saint Augustine, Florida, to defend gold bullion ships returning to Spain

1584–1587 English establish a colony on Roanoke Island

1600

1607 Jamestown is founded
1608 Samuel de Champlain founds Québec
1610–1611 Henry Hudson fails to find the Northwest Passage to the Pacific Ocean
1613 French begin fur trading around the Great Lakes
1619 Dutch import the first 20 African slaves to Virginia
1620 Pilgrim Fathers arrive in Plymouth
1626 Dutch buy Manhattan Island
1630–1670 French Jesuits explore the Great Lakes

1650

1664 British acquire New Amsterdam from the Dutch and rename it New York
1670 English set up Hudson's Bay Co. to trade furs in northern Canada
1671 English explorers Batts and Fallam are the first Europeans to cross the Appalachian Mountains into the Ohio river valley
1681–1682 Robert de la Salle canoes down the full length of the Mississippi river
1681–1682 William Penn founds Pennsylvania
1686–1690 Spanish explore Texas

1700

1713 Britain gains Nova Scotia and Newfoundland from France

1731 French start fur trade around Lake Winnipeg

1750

1755–1763 French and Indian War against the British
1759 General Wolfe seizes Québec
1760 Baron Amherst seizes Montréal, ending French control of Canada
1763 Treaty of Paris gives French Canada to Britain and Louisiana to Spain

1800

The age of absolutism

In the mid-1600s a series of strong monarchs emerged in Europe. They held complete control and believed in "absolutism," the idea that the power of the state was embodied in the king, who did not have to answer to anyone. The greatest of these monarchs was Louis XIV of France, who famously said, "*L'état, c'est moi*" ("I am the state"). Under Louis XIV, France fought a series of wars against the Hapsburgs of Spain and Austria to become the most powerful state in Europe by 1715. To the east, Prussia began to emerge as the strongest state in Germany, while Austria fought off its many enemies to become the leading state in central Europe by 1750.

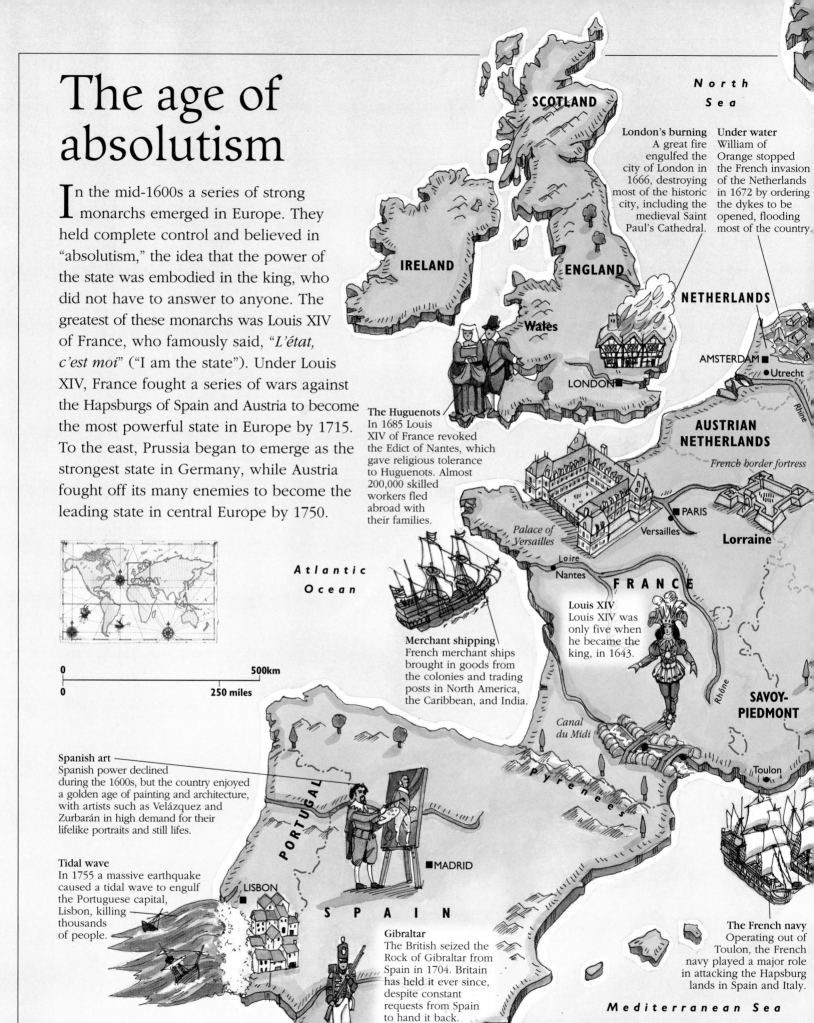

North Sea

SCOTLAND

London's burning
A great fire engulfed the city of London in 1666, destroying most of the historic city, including the medieval Saint Paul's Cathedral.

Under water
William of Orange stopped the French invasion of the Netherlands in 1672 by ordering the dykes to be opened, flooding most of the country.

IRELAND

ENGLAND

Wales

NETHERLANDS

AMSTERDAM ■
● Utrecht

The Huguenots
In 1685 Louis XIV of France revoked the Edict of Nantes, which gave religious tolerance to Huguenots. Almost 200,000 skilled workers fled abroad with their families.

LONDON ■

AUSTRIAN NETHERLANDS

French border fortress

Rhine

PARIS ■
Versailles

Palace of Versailles

Lorraine

Atlantic Ocean

Loire
● Nantes

F R A N C E

Louis XIV
Louis XIV was only five when he became the king, in 1643.

Merchant shipping
French merchant ships brought in goods from the colonies and trading posts in North America, the Caribbean, and India.

Rhône

SAVOY-PIEDMONT

Canal du Midi

0 _____ 500km
0 _____ 250 miles

Spanish art
Spanish power declined during the 1600s, but the country enjoyed a golden age of painting and architecture, with artists such as Velázquez and Zurbarán in high demand for their lifelike portraits and still lifes.

P y r e n e e s

Toulon
●

Tidal wave
In 1755 a massive earthquake caused a tidal wave to engulf the Portuguese capital, Lisbon, killing thousands of people.

LISBON

MADRID ■

S P A I N

Gibraltar
The British seized the Rock of Gibraltar from Spain in 1704. Britain has held it ever since, despite constant requests from Spain to hand it back.

The French navy
Operating out of Toulon, the French navy played a major role in attacking the Hapsburg lands in Spain and Italy.

Mediterranean Sea

Gibraltar

SWEDEN

DENMARK – NORWAY

Baltic Sea

PRUSSIA

POLAND

Prussian troops
After 1640 Prussia slowly emerged as the largest state in northern Germany, ruled by a series of excellent kings and protected by a powerful army.

● Hanover

HOLY ROMAN EMPIRE

George of Hanover
In 1714 the Duke of Hanover, a minor German state, became the king of Great Britain when he succeeded his distant cousin, Queen Anne.

Vistula

Elbe

GERMANY

Polish harvests
Constant invasions devastated the grain fields of Poland during the 1750s, leading to a population decline and eventually the collapse of the country itself.

Duke of Marlborough
As the leader of the anti-French armies during the War of the Spanish Succession, the duke achieved great victories in Blenheim and elsewhere.

Blenheim

Schönbrunn Palace
Maria Theresa saved her bankrupt Austrian Empire from collapse during the 1740s. She ruled over a glittering court from her palace outside of Vienna.

VIENNA

AUSTRIA

Danube

A
L
P
S

Serfs
In Austria serfs (peasants) were owned by their landlords and were not legally freed from serfdom until 1781. Many remained tied to this kind of servitude until the 1840s.

this dotted line shows the full extent of the Holy Roman Empire in 1780

these dotted lines show other national borders in Europe in 1780

VENICE

Genoa

GENOA

Corsica

ROME

NAPLES

The Pope
Although still an important ruler in Italy, the Pope's religious and political power in the rest of Europe was minimal at this time.

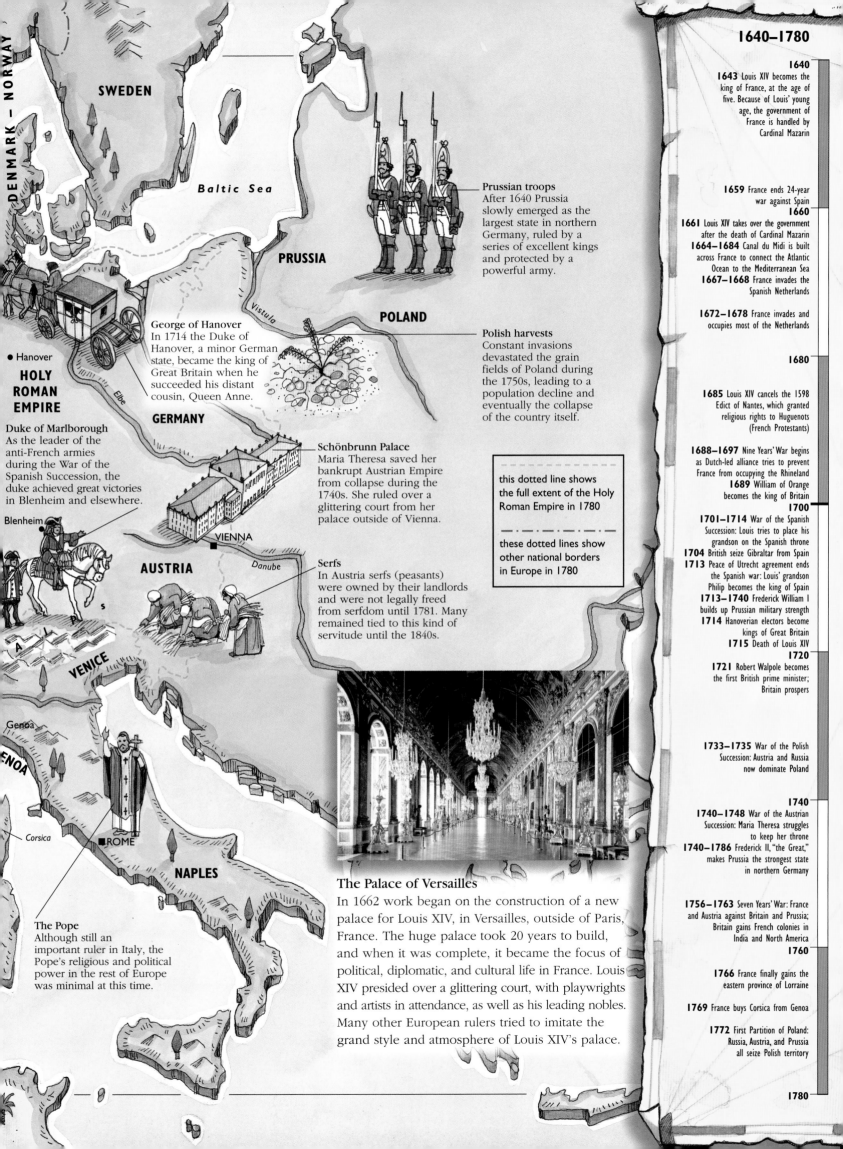

The Palace of Versailles

In 1662 work began on the construction of a new palace for Louis XIV, in Versailles, outside of Paris, France. The huge palace took 20 years to build, and when it was complete, it became the focus of political, diplomatic, and cultural life in France. Louis XIV presided over a glittering court, with playwrights and artists in attendance, as well as his leading nobles. Many other European rulers tried to imitate the grand style and atmosphere of Louis XIV's palace.

1640–1780

1640

1643 Louis XIV becomes the king of France, at the age of five. Because of Louis' young age, the government of France is handled by Cardinal Mazarin

1659 France ends 24-year war against Spain
1660
1661 Louis XIV takes over the government after the death of Cardinal Mazarin
1664–1684 Canal du Midi is built across France to connect the Atlantic Ocean to the Mediterranean Sea
1667–1668 France invades the Spanish Netherlands

1672–1678 France invades and occupies most of the Netherlands

1680

1685 Louis XIV cancels the 1598 Edict of Nantes, which granted religious rights to Huguenots (French Protestants)

1688–1697 Nine Years' War begins as Dutch-led alliance tries to prevent France from occupying the Rhineland
1689 William of Orange becomes the king of Britain
1700
1701–1714 War of the Spanish Succession: Louis tries to place his grandson on the Spanish throne
1704 British seize Gibraltar from Spain
1713 Peace of Utrecht agreement ends the Spanish war: Louis' grandson Philip becomes the king of Spain
1713–1740 Frederick William I builds up Prussian military strength
1714 Hanoverian electors become kings of Great Britain
1715 Death of Louis XIV
1720
1721 Robert Walpole becomes the first British prime minister; Britain prospers

1733–1735 War of the Polish Succession: Austria and Russia now dominate Poland

1740
1740–1748 War of the Austrian Succession: Maria Theresa struggles to keep her throne
1740–1786 Frederick II, "the Great," makes Prussia the strongest state in northern Germany

1756–1763 Seven Years' War: France and Austria against Britain and Prussia; Britain gains French colonies in India and North America
1760

1766 France finally gains the eastern province of Lorraine

1769 France buys Corsica from Genoa

1772 First Partition of Poland: Russia, Austria, and Prussia all seize Polish territory

1780

The intellectual revolution:
An enlightened view of the world

During the mid-1600s, a new way of looking at the world began to flourish in Europe. This movement is known as the Enlightenment because it was a time of new ideas based on human logic and reason, rather than on the old religious beliefs of the Christian Church. The Enlightenment had a huge impact not just on philosophy and politics, but also on science and invention. The Enlightenment movement was opposed by the Catholic Church, but some rulers supported these new ideas, setting up universities and scientific societies and granting religious and political freedom to their subjects.

Politics

The Enlightenment changed political thinking and influenced the French Revolution of 1789. In 1791–1792 the English pamphlet-writer Thomas Paine (1737–1809, right) wrote *The Rights of Man*, in support of the revolution, but he was forced to flee to France. There he wrote *The Age of Reason* (1795), attacking Christianity, and was almost executed by guillotine.

Philosophy

The French philosopher René Descartes (1596–1650, left) is often seen as the founder of modern philosophy, putting logic and reason at the center of his thinking. He summed up his beliefs in the phrase, "I think, therefore I am." Around 100 years later Voltaire (1694–1778) wrote a series of witty pamphlets, novels, and plays that were read by people all across Europe, making the new ideas of the Enlightenment very popular.

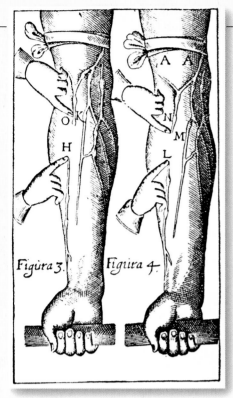

Anatomy

In 1628 William Harvey published
De Motu Cordis—"On the Motion of
the Heart"—in which he suggested
that blood is pumped by the heart
and that it is constantly circulating
around the body. His explanations
overturned medical beliefs that
had been followed since the
Greeks, 1,400 years earlier.

Physics

The English scientist Isaac Newton
(1642–1727, right) demonstrated
that white light is made up of a
spectrum of colors. He did this by
"refracting" the light through a
glass prism. Most importantly,
he defined the three laws of
motion and the law of universal
gravitation—the invisible force
of attraction between objects.

*Eyepiece lens turns
image the right way up*

*Lenses magnify subject
around 21 times, which
allowed Galileo to only see
one third of the Moon at
a time*

Astronomy

Both Galileo Galilei (1564–1642) and
Johannes Kepler (1571–1630) developed
the basic ideas of Nicolaus Copernicus
(see page 14). Galileo invented a telescope
for studying the movement of the planets.
Kepler discovered that the planets move
around the Sun in ellipses (ovals) rather
than in circles and that they move fastest
when they are closest to the Sun.

*Object lens
magnifies subject
but turns it
upside down*

Microscopy

Robert Hooke (1635–1703) developed
a powerful "compound," or multilens,
microscope (left) for studying very
small organisms. He was the first
person to use the word "cell"
to describe the tiny units out of
which all living things are made.

*Galileo used this telescope
to view the sky in 1609. The
telescope gives a restricted view
because the lenses are small.*

*Ornamental stand
for the telescope*

Exploring the Pacific Ocean

KEY TO VOYAGES

Ferdinand Magellan	1519–1521
Alvaro de Mendaña	1567–1569
Abel Tasman	1642–1643
James Cook: 1st voyage	1768–1771

The first Europeans entered the Pacific Ocean in the 1500s, looking for a new sea route to Asia and its riches. In the 1600s merchants came in search of spices, setting up trading posts throughout the East Indies (Indonesia). Many islands in the Pacific Ocean remained unknown to Europeans, as did Australia, which Dutch navigators either mistook for New Guinea or sailed right past. It was not until 1770 that Captain Cook made an actual landing there. Eighteen years later 750 British convicts became the first permanent European settlers in Australia.

Crossing the Pacific Ocean
Magellan took four months to cross the Pacific Ocean. He landed in Guam and then eventually reached the Philippines, where he was killed in a skirmish with local people.

Pacific trade
Spanish galleons regularly crossed the Pacific Ocean, taking silver from Acapulco, Mexico, and returning from Manila, in the Philippines, with Chinese silk.

Silk trade
Portuguese merchants based in Macao supplied fine Chinese silk to the Spanish in the Philippines.

Macao

CHINA

PHILIPPINES

Mining tin

South China Sea

Manila

Spanish Catholic church

Guam

Cannibals
Mendaña sent some of his crew ashore in the Solomon Islands to find freshwater. They were attacked by cannibals.

Malay Peninsula

Malacca

Gold ore
Aborigines in Borneo

Cloves

Ternate

Polynesians fishing

SOLOMON ISLANDS

Pepper

EAST INDIES

Sumatra

Moluccas Islands

Amboina

Banda Islands

Tasman trading with natives

Reefed
Captain Cook ran his ship *Endeavour* aground on the Great Barrier Reef. He and his crew had to stop to repair the large hole in the ship's hull.

Indian Ocean

BATAVIA

Sugar

Java

Solor

Kupang

Timor

Coffee

Nutmeg

New Guinea

FIJI

TONGA

Batavia
Batavia was the headquarters of the Dutch East Indies Company, a trading organization that dominated the spice trade in the region.

Malacca
The Portuguese built a large fort in Malacca so that they could dominate the sea route between the Indian Ocean and the South China Sea.

AUSTRALIA

Great Barrier Reef

Aborigines
Around 300,000 Aborigines lived in Australia before the Europeans arrived. Their numbers dropped after foreign settlement began, because of diseases and violence brought in by the settlers.

Botany Bay
The first 750 British convicts landed in Botany Bay in 1788 to serve their prison sentences in Australia. 160,000 more followed until this practice was stopped in 1868.

Botany Bay

A ship from Abel Tasman's fleet

Tasmania

North Island

NEW ZEALAND

South Island

Tasmania
Tasman sent a carpenter ashore to plant a flag on what he called Van Diemen's Land, named after the governor-general of Dutch Batavia. The island is now called Tasmania, after Tasman himself.

Brutal welcome
When Captain Cook landed on the North Island of New Zealand, he and his crew were attacked by the native Maori people. In the skirmish several Maori were shot.

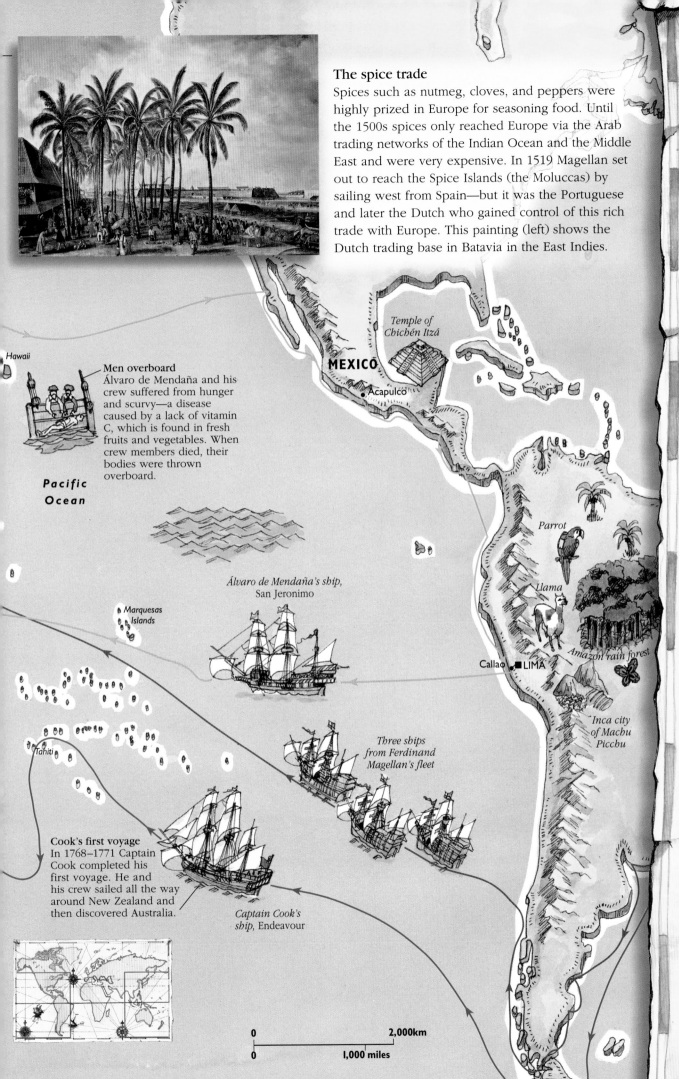

The spice trade

Spices such as nutmeg, cloves, and peppers were highly prized in Europe for seasoning food. Until the 1500s spices only reached Europe via the Arab trading networks of the Indian Ocean and the Middle East and were very expensive. In 1519 Magellan set out to reach the Spice Islands (the Moluccas) by sailing west from Spain—but it was the Portuguese and later the Dutch who gained control of this rich trade with Europe. This painting (left) shows the Dutch trading base in Batavia in the East Indies.

Hawaii

Men overboard
Álvaro de Mendaña and his crew suffered from hunger and scurvy—a disease caused by a lack of vitamin C, which is found in fresh fruits and vegetables. When crew members died, their bodies were thrown overboard.

Pacific Ocean

Temple of Chichén Itzá

MEXICO
• Acapulco

Parrot

Llama

Amazon rain forest

Callao ■ LIMA

Álvaro de Mendaña's ship, San Jeronimo

Marquesas Islands

Inca city of Machu Picchu

Tahiti

Three ships from Ferdinand Magellan's fleet

Cook's first voyage
In 1768–1771 Captain Cook completed his first voyage. He and his crew sailed all the way around New Zealand and then discovered Australia.

Captain Cook's ship, Endeavour

| 0 | | 2,000km |
| 0 | | 1,000 miles |

1500

1511 Portuguese seize Malacca and Malay Peninsula

1520–1521 Ferdinand Magellan crosses the Pacific Ocean, the first European to do so

1567–1569 Álvaro de Mendaña explores the South Pacific Ocean and discovers the Solomon Islands
1571 Spanish found Manila as the capital of the Philippines
1579 Francis Drake crosses the Pacific Ocean from California to the Philippines

1595–1596 Álvaro de Mendaña dies in an attempt to set up a Spanish colony in the Solomon Islands
1596 First arrival of the Dutch in Java
1600
1602 Dutch East Indies Co. is founded
1605–1606 Dutch navigator Willem Jantszoon explores the north coast of Australia but thinks that it is part of New Guinea
1606–1607 Luis de Torres sails around New Guinea, proving that it is an island

1619 Dutch seize Batavia and set up Dutch East Indies Co. headquarters there
1623 Dutch drive British out of the Spice Islands (Moluccas)
1629 Dutch drive Portuguese out of the Spice Islands

1641 Dutch seize Malacca from the Portuguese
1642–1643 Abel Tasman discovers Van Diemen's Land (Tasmania), New Zealand, Fiji, and Tonga

1667 Dutch complete their conquest of the Spice Islands

1684 Dutch seize most of Java and eastern Sumatra

1700
1700 Dutch dominate European trade with the East Indies (Indonesia)

1768–1771 Cook's first voyage: he circumnavigates (sails around) New Zealand and discovers Australia
1772–1775 Cook's second voyage: he explores Antarctica
1776–1779 Cook's third voyage: he sails north, to find an inlet into the Arctic Ocean, and discovers Hawaii, where he dies

1788 First British convicts land in Botany Bay, Australia
1792 First British settlement in New Zealand

1800

The American Revolutionary War

In 1775 all 13 of the British colonies in North America rose up in revolt. They protested against British attempts to restrict their freedom and to tax them without giving them any representation in Parliament. Led by George Washington, and later supported by the French, the colonists declared their independence in 1776 and won a series of military victories before the war ended in 1783. This victory gave birth to a new nation, the United States of America, which initially only stretched as far inland as the Mississippi river. Eventually, it extended all the way across the continent, to the Pacific Ocean in the west.

George Washington
George Washington (1732–1799) was a colonial farmer in Virginia who fought for the British against the French in the 1750s. He was the ideal person to command the American forces against the British and led them to victory in 1781. As the first president of the newly independent United States, from 1789–1797, he led the nation with great skill and determination.

The Boston Tea Party
Colonists who were upset by the British government's tax on imported tea dumped a cargo of tea into Boston Harbor in 1773.

Paul Revere
On April 18, 1775, silversmith Paul Revere rode through the night to warn people that British troops were coming to capture military supplies in Concord.

Loyalists
Americans from New York and South Carolina, who were loyal to the British crown, fled north to Canada along with the Mohawks who had fought for the British. They settled in Ontario and the provinces close to the sea.

Saratoga
A British attempt to isolate the New England colonies from the rest of America was defeated in Saratoga in 1777.

The legend of Betsy Ross
Betsy Ross was asked to make the first American flag using six-pointed stars, but she said that five-pointed stars "would look better."

Crossing the Delaware
On Christmas Day in 1776 George Washington led his recently defeated army across the icy Delaware river, surprising the British and winning a crucial battle in Trenton.

A new capital
In 1791 the decision was made to build a new national capital on the Potomac river. It was named "Washington" in honor of the first president, George Washington.

CANADA

Québec

Montréal

Saratoga

New Hampshire
Concord
Bunker Hill
Lexington
Boston
Massachusetts
Rhode Island
Connecticut

New York
Hudson
New York
Princeton
Trenton
Philadelphia
Brandywine
Pennsylvania
Delaware
New Jersey
Baltimore
WASHINGTON

Appalachian Mountains

Lake Ontario
Lake Erie

Ontario

Lake Huron

Lake Michigan

Lake Superior

Mississippi

UNITED STATES OF AMERICA

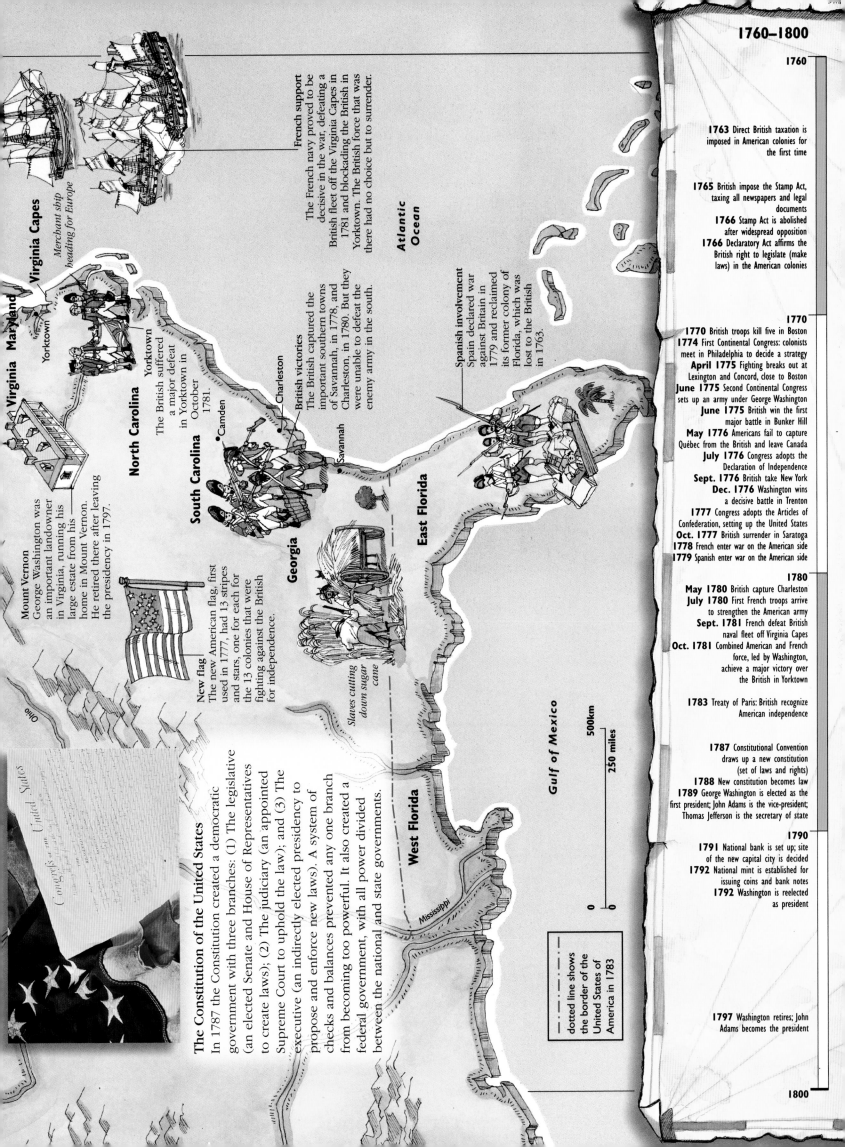

The Constitution of the United States

In 1787 the Constitution created a democratic government with three branches: (1) The legislative (an elected Senate and House of Representatives to create laws); (2) The judiciary (an appointed Supreme Court to uphold the law); and (3) The executive (an indirectly elected presidency to propose and enforce new laws). A system of checks and balances prevented any one branch from becoming too powerful. It also created a federal government, with all power divided between the national and state governments.

Mount Vernon
George Washington was an important landowner in Virginia, running his large estate from his home in Mount Vernon. He retired there after leaving the presidency in 1797.

New flag
The new American flag, first used in 1777, had 13 stripes and stars, one for each of the 13 colonies that were fighting against the British for independence.

Virginia Capes

Merchant ship heading for Europe

French support
The French navy proved to be decisive in the war, defeating a British fleet off the Virginia Capes in 1781 and blockading the British in Yorktown. The British force that was there had no choice but to surrender.

Maryland

Virginia

Yorktown

North Carolina

Yorktown
The British suffered a major defeat in Yorktown in October 1781.

Camden

South Carolina

Charleston

British victories
The British captured the important southern towns of Savannah, in 1778, and Charleston, in 1780. But they were unable to defeat the enemy army in the south.

Savannah

Georgia

Slaves cutting down sugar cane

East Florida

Spanish involvement
Spain declared war against Britain in 1779 and reclaimed its former colony of Florida, which was lost to the British in 1763.

Atlantic Ocean

Gulf of Mexico

West Florida

Mississippi

Ohio

500km

250 miles

0

0

--- · --- dotted line shows the border of the United States of America in 1783

1760

1763 Direct British taxation is imposed in American colonies for the first time

1765 British impose the Stamp Act, taxing all newspapers and legal documents
1766 Stamp Act is abolished after widespread opposition
1766 Declaratory Act affirms the British right to legislate (make laws) in the American colonies

1770

1770 British troops kill five in Boston
1774 First Continental Congress: colonists meet in Philadelphia to decide a strategy
April 1775 Fighting breaks out at Lexington and Concord, close to Boston
June 1775 Second Continental Congress sets up an army under George Washington
June 1775 British win the first major battle in Bunker Hill
May 1776 Americans fail to capture Québec from the British and leave Canada
July 1776 Congress adopts the Declaration of Independence
Sept. 1776 British take New York
Dec. 1776 Washington wins a decisive battle in Trenton
1777 Congress adopts the Articles of Confederation, setting up the United States
Oct. 1777 British surrender in Saratoga
1778 French enter war on the American side
1779 Spanish enter war on the American side

1780

May 1780 British capture Charleston
July 1780 First French troops arrive to strengthen the American army
Sept. 1781 French defeat British naval fleet off Virginia Capes
Oct. 1781 Combined American and French force, led by Washington, achieve a major victory over the British in Yorktown

1783 Treaty of Paris: British recognize American independence

1787 Constitutional Convention draws up a new constitution (set of laws and rights)
1788 New constitution becomes law
1789 George Washington is elected as the first president; John Adams is the vice-president; Thomas Jefferson is the secretary of state

1790

1791 National bank is set up; site of the new capital city is decided
1792 National mint is established for issuing coins and bank notes
1792 Washington is reelected as president

1797 Washington retires; John Adams becomes the president

1800

The French Revolution

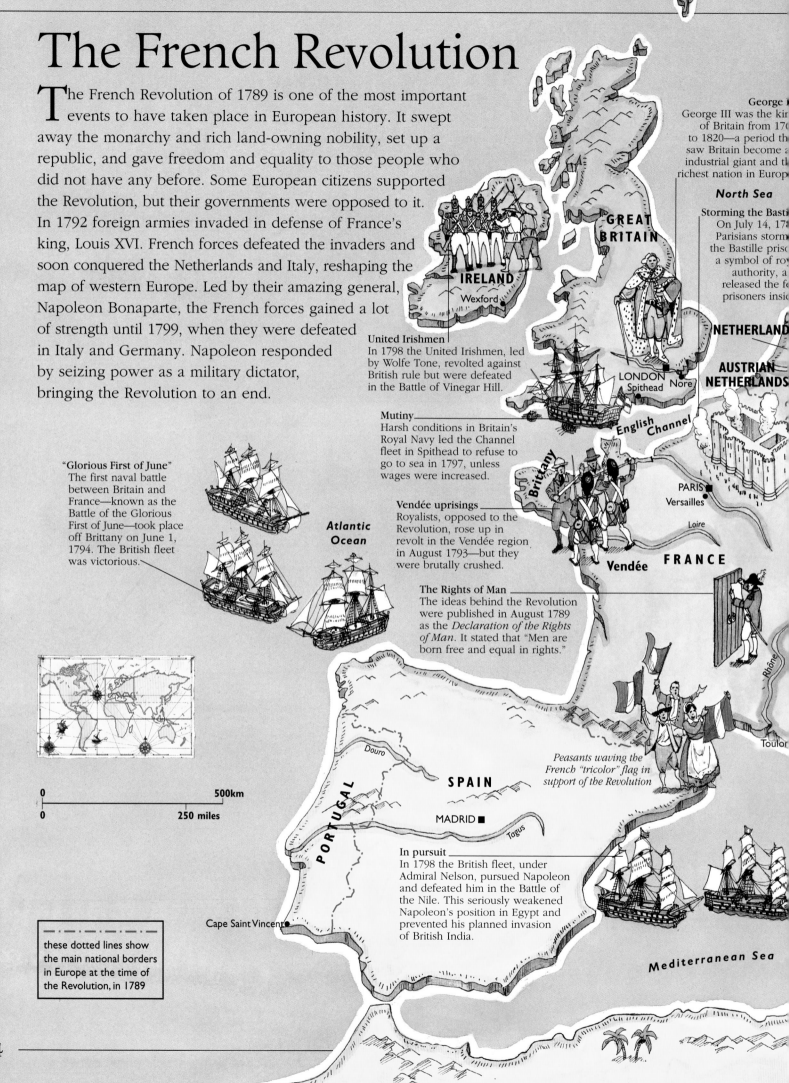

T he French Revolution of 1789 is one of the most important events to have taken place in European history. It swept away the monarchy and rich land-owning nobility, set up a republic, and gave freedom and equality to those people who did not have any before. Some European citizens supported the Revolution, but their governments were opposed to it. In 1792 foreign armies invaded in defense of France's king, Louis XVI. French forces defeated the invaders and soon conquered the Netherlands and Italy, reshaping the map of western Europe. Led by their amazing general, Napoleon Bonaparte, the French forces gained a lot of strength until 1799, when they were defeated in Italy and Germany. Napoleon responded by seizing power as a military dictator, bringing the Revolution to an end.

George I
George III was the kin of Britain from 176 to 1820—a period th saw Britain become a industrial giant and th richest nation in Europ

North Sea

Storming the Basti
On July 14, 178 Parisians storm the Bastille priso a symbol of roy authority, a released the fe prisoners insid

NETHERLAND

AUSTRIAN NETHERLANDS

GREAT BRITAIN

IRELAND
Wexford

LONDON
Spithead Nore

United Irishmen
In 1798 the United Irishmen, led by Wolfe Tone, revolted against British rule but were defeated in the Battle of Vinegar Hill.

Mutiny
Harsh conditions in Britain's Royal Navy led the Channel fleet in Spithead to refuse to go to sea in 1797, unless wages were increased.

English Channel

Brittany

PARIS
Versailles

Loire

"Glorious First of June"
The first naval battle between Britain and France—known as the Battle of the Glorious First of June—took place off Brittany on June 1, 1794. The British fleet was victorious.

Atlantic Ocean

Vendée uprisings
Royalists, opposed to the Revolution, rose up in revolt in the Vendée region in August 1793—but they were brutally crushed.

Vendée FRANCE

The Rights of Man
The ideas behind the Revolution were published in August 1789 as the *Declaration of the Rights of Man*. It stated that "Men are born free and equal in rights."

Rhône

Peasants waving the French "tricolor" flag in support of the Revolution

Douro

SPAIN

MADRID

Tagus

Toulo

0   500km
0   250 miles

In pursuit
In 1798 the British fleet, under Admiral Nelson, pursued Napoleon and defeated him in the Battle of the Nile. This seriously weakened Napoleon's position in Egypt and prevented his planned invasion of British India.

PORTUGAL

Cape Saint Vincent

Mediterranean Sea

these dotted lines show the main national borders in Europe at the time of the Revolution, in 1789

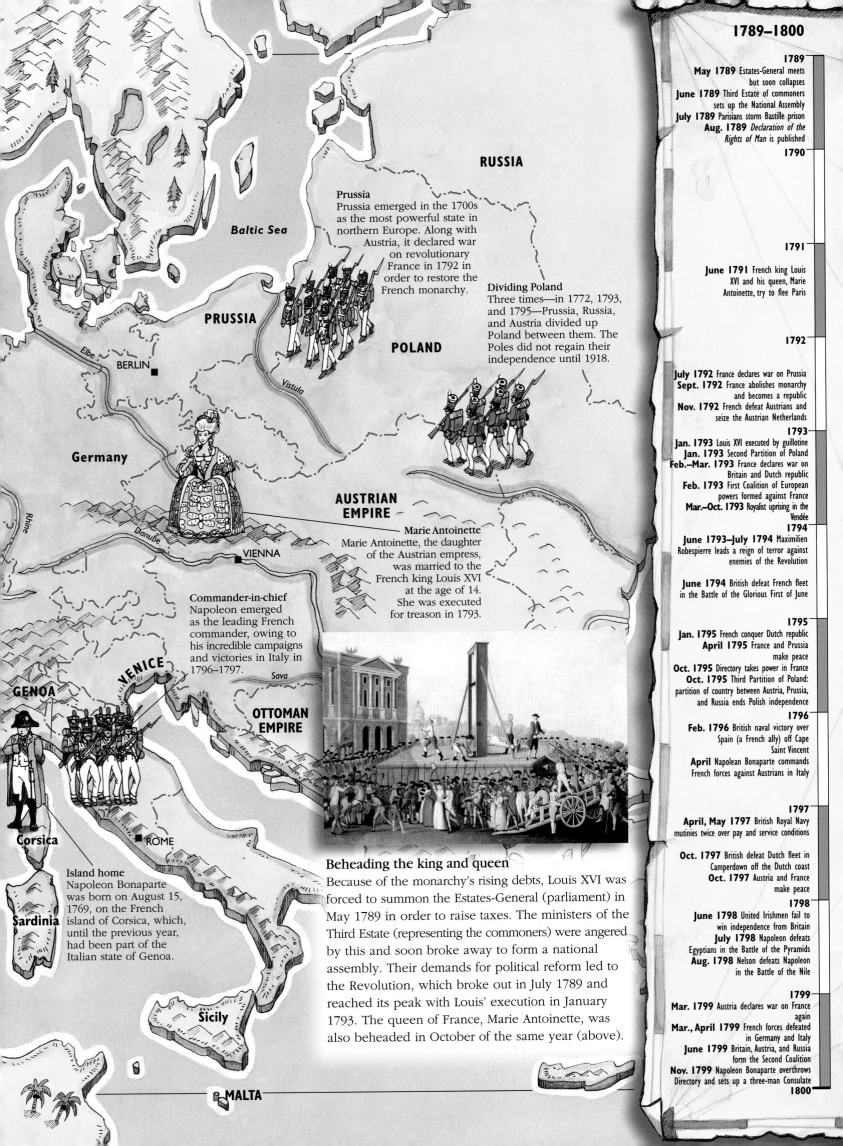

RUSSIA

Baltic Sea

Prussia
Prussia emerged in the 1700s as the most powerful state in northern Europe. Along with Austria, it declared war on revolutionary France in 1792 in order to restore the French monarchy.

PRUSSIA

Dividing Poland
Three times—in 1772, 1793, and 1795—Prussia, Russia, and Austria divided up Poland between them. The Poles did not regain their independence until 1918.

POLAND

Elbe

BERLIN

Vistula

Germany

Rhine

Danube

AUSTRIAN EMPIRE

Marie Antoinette
Marie Antoinette, the daughter of the Austrian empress, was married to the French king Louis XVI at the age of 14. She was executed for treason in 1793.

VIENNA

Commander-in-chief
Napoleon emerged as the leading French commander, owing to his incredible campaigns and victories in Italy in 1796–1797.

Sava

VENICE

GENOA

OTTOMAN EMPIRE

Corsica

ROME

Island home
Napoleon Bonaparte was born on August 15, 1769, on the French island of Corsica, which, until the previous year, had been part of the Italian state of Genoa.

Sardinia

Sicily

MALTA

Beheading the king and queen

Because of the monarchy's rising debts, Louis XVI was forced to summon the Estates-General (parliament) in May 1789 in order to raise taxes. The ministers of the Third Estate (representing the commoners) were angered by this and soon broke away to form a national assembly. Their demands for political reform led to the Revolution, which broke out in July 1789 and reached its peak with Louis' execution in January 1793. The queen of France, Marie Antoinette, was also beheaded in October of the same year (above).

Index

This index lists the main peoples, places, and topics that you will find in the text in this book. It is not a full index of all of the place names and physical features that are found on the maps.

Acknowledgments

The publisher would like to thank the following for permission to reproduce their material.
Every care has been taken to trace copyright holders. However, if there have been
unintentional omissions or failure to trace copyright holders, we apologize and
will, if informed, endeavor to make corrections in any future edition.

Key: *b* = bottom, *c* = center, *l* = left, *r* = right, *t* = top

Pages 6*cl* Bridgeman Art Library, London/Capitol Collection, Washington; 6–7*b* Corbis/Svenja-Foto Zefa;
6*tr* Bridgeman Art Library/Universitäts Bibliothek, Göttingen; 7*tl* The Art Archive/Culver Pictures; 7*tr* The
Art Archive/Gunshots; 9*tl* Bridgeman Art Library/The National Maritime Museum, U.K.; 11*bl* The Art Archive;
12*tl* Corbis/Gianni Dagli Orti; 13*bl* The Art Archive/Archivo des Indias, Seville; 14*tl* Science & Society Picture
Library; 14*cl* Bridgeman Art Library/British Library, London; 14*br* Bridgeman Art Library/Galleria dell'Academia,
Florence; 15*tl* Bridgeman Art Library/Museo degli Argenti, Palazzo Pitti, Florence; 17*tr* Bridgeman Art
Library/Private Collection; 17*br* Photolibrary/The Travel Library Ltd.; 19*tr* The Art Archive/Museum der
Stadt Wien/Dagli Orti; 21*b* British Museum; 21*tl* Photolibrary/Jon Arnold Images; 22*tl* The Art Archive;
25*tr* Corbis/Keren Su; 25*br* Bridgeman Art Library/Royal Library, Sweden; 28*bl* Bridgeman Art Library/Private
Collection; 31*tl* Corbis/Werner Forman; 32*tr* Bridgeman Art Library/Bibliotheque des Artes Decoratifs, Paris;
32*b* The Art Archive; 33*bl* Corbis/Tony Arruzza; 33*br* The Art Archive; 34*l* Corbis/Burstein Collection;
37*br* Corbis/Massimo Listri; 38*l* The Art Archive/Institut de France, Paris; 38*r* Bridgeman Art Library/British
Library; 39*tl* Science Photo Library/Dr. Jeremy Burgess; 39*bl* Science & Society Picture Library; 39*tr* Science
Photo Library; 39*br* Scala/Museo della Scienze, Florence; 41*tl* Bridgeman Art Library/Rijksmuseum, Amsterdam;
42*tl* Corbis/Christie's Images; 45*r* Corbis/Gianni Dagli Orti.

All illustrations by Mark Bergin.

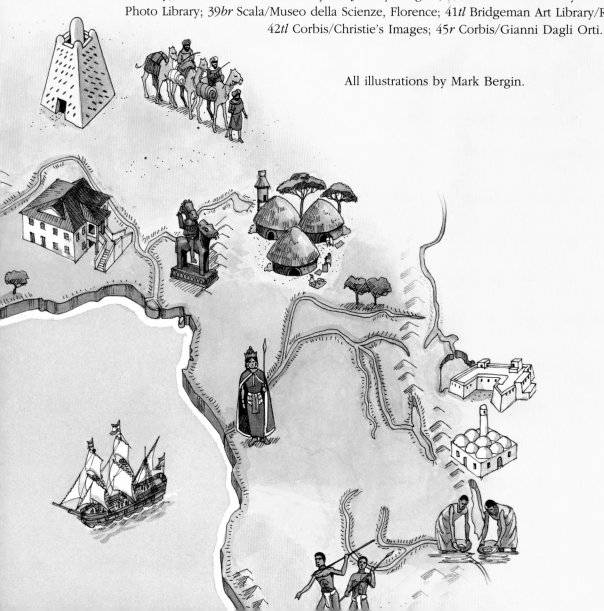